The Reluctant Nurse

Rosemary Rowley

Published by

MELROSE
   BOOKS
An Imprint of Melrose Press Limited
St Thomas Place, Ely
Cambridgeshire
CB7 4GG, UK
www.melrosebooks.com

FIRST EDITION

Copyright © Rosemary Rowley 2005

The Author asserts her moral right to
be identified as the author of this work

Cover designed by Bryan Carpenter

ISBN 1 905226 29 2

Printed and bound in Great Britain by:
Bath Press Limited, Lower Bristol Road,
Bath, BA2 3BL, UK

The Reluctant Nurse

Rosemary Rowley

Chapter 1

Early Days

My parents, Edward Harry and Margaret Elizabeth Rowley, were married on 31 July 1928 at Holy Trinity Church, Kingston-upon-Hull. They had met about 12 years previously at a confirmation class, when they were both aged 16. They became engaged 2 years later. This long engagement was fairly typical then, as it gave couples time to be in a fit financial state to marry. My mother was required to give up her teaching career on marriage, but by then, my father had secured promotion at work in the local tar distillery, from Office Boy to Company Secretary. He was a bright lad but had had to leave school early, despite showing promise, because his father had died when he was 9, leaving his mother, who was over 40 when she married, to bring up Eddie and his older brother George. During their long engagement, he attended night school learning Greek, among other things.

In the early days of their marriage, they lived with my maternal grandparents in Anlaby, a suburb of Hull. My brother Patrick was born on 9 July 1929. My mother told me many years later how difficult his birth had been. She was in labour at home for 2 days and she showed me the huckaback towel which had been tied to the end of the bed for her to pull on. The creases were worn into it. He was delivered by forceps with great difficulty. Initially, his life was despaired of, as it was again, more than once, during his childhood.

My arrival, in the middle of a thunderstorm on a Sunday afternoon on 25 October 1931, was a great deal easier and I presented few problems during my infancy. Apparently, I was a very placid baby and would lie in my cot, quietly moving my fingers up and down. They thought I might become a concert pianist but they could not have been more wrong.

5

By the time I was born, my family lived in a house called "Chevin" in Pickering Road. It was so called after the hill near Ilkley where my parents had spent their honeymoon. Opposite the house was a park, with a sandpit, swings, roundabouts and a boating lake. One of my earliest memories is being brought home by the park keeper, naked and wet, with a little boy who lived nearby. We had taken off all our clothes and gone paddling in the lake.

Patrick and I had most of the childhood diseases and I tended to suffer from croup. He was thought at one time to have bronchiectasis – a disease which seems to have disappeared. One spring, when I was 3, I had chickenpox and I remember 5 tiny kittens being brought in on a wooden tray for me to see. I was allowed to choose one and I called it "Bluebell" because of the flowers in my bedroom. We also had a black Labrador called "Duke" and his kennel was a tar barrel, with one side removed, in the garden. We had a garage and a playroom had been built over it, which was paradise for 2 small children. One of my delights was making mud pies, but my mother was none too pleased when she discovered that I had "borrowed" her jam tart tins and then decorated the pies with her best glace cherries.

My maternal grandmother, now widowed, came to live with us about this time and to me she seemed to be a very old lady. She was barely 60. Every Saturday, she gave us both a penny for sweets – one could buy 40 aniseed balls for a penny in those days or 10 for a farthing! After some months, she had a stroke and became bed-bound until she died some weeks later. I was not quite 5 when she died and as she was the last of my grandparents, I shall always regret missing out on the support, benefit and love I might have had.

During those early days of childhood, I felt loved and secure but I have few memories of "Chevin" before we moved in 1936. However, some things stand out. I clearly recall being taken outside to see a Zeppelin passing overhead and I also remember sitting alone at the bottom of the garden among the flowers pondering about the meaning of life. But one of my sharpest memories is of the day we went to London when I was 4 years old. I was very excited about this trip and I woke up very early, before anyone else. I went downstairs, and with great difficulty reached up to put on the kitchen light. I knew that one of the first things my father did in the morning was shave, so I found his razor (not a cut-throat!) and did quite a good job of removing skin from my chin before I was discovered. I went to London bearing a

The Wedding, 31 July 1928.
Margaret Elizabeth Clark and Edward Harry Rowley.

Patrick, Rosemary and Duke

My parents in the USA, 1930.
(Father on right).

plaster. We travelled by train, the four of us and Auntie Mary, who was not really an aunt but a distant relative by marriage. The object of the journey was for my parents to view a motor car which they had seen advertised and Auntie Mary's job was to bear us children off to the Zoo. We had a great time looking at the animals and finally having a ride on an elephant. After I had been lifted down from a great height, I was allowed to give the elephant a bun, and it was splendid to watch this magnificent beast gently lift up the bun with his trunk and put it in his mouth.

My parents, meanwhile, had viewed the car, and bought it! It was a showroom model, with very few miles on the clock – a green and black Singer with the registration AXP 479. Throughout her life, my mother was superstitious about that number, considering it to be lucky. Before her marriage, she had had a motorbike and was therefore very well known to all the policemen on point duty in Hull – she was said to be the first woman in Hull to have a motorbike. Quite a lot of courting was done on that bike, my father riding pillion. My mother therefore had no fear of a car and drove us all back to Hull in it. It did not have a heater, of course, or windscreen wipers. Later, Patrick and I travelled in the back, with rugs and stone hot water bottles, being asked general knowledge questions from a red book compiled by George A. Birmingham. My mother was a fearless driver (it was the passengers who showed fear!) and during her long life drove many cars many thousands of miles. Pa also had a licence but as she had the more forceful personality, he preferred to let her drive.

In 1936, the decision was made for us to move. Patrick had had several periods of ill health and it was thought that he would be better on higher ground. So a plot of land, 5 miles out of Hull and fairly near the village of Hessle, was bought and the services of an architect sought. The house, known as St. Hilary (the Patron Saint of Mirth and Laughter), was duly designed and built, very much in the 30s style – all square and windows. The land had belonged to the Tranby Park Estate and it was in Tranby Croft on the Estate that King Edward VII had been accused of cheating at cards.

We had a large plot of land behind the house which gave Ma great scope in planning vegetable plots and flower beds. Inside, there was an integral garage and a kitchen with an AGA cooker. The lounge and dining rooms both had open fires and the main bedroom had a gas fire. My room had a balcony and looked out over the main road to a golf course. Beyond that, in winter when the trees were bare, one could catch a glimpse of the River Humber.

In September 1937, when I was almost 6, my education began at St. Mary's Convent in Hull. It was a Roman Catholic school which accepted Anglicans, although we were not allowed to attend morning prayers. In the kindergarten, however, which was in the care of a delightful and gentle nun called Sister Mary Gerard, we said the Lord's Prayer together every morning, no doubt to get us into the right frame of mind. Only once that year was I in disgrace and I had to go up to the front of the class to have my hand slapped with a ruler. I did not know how I had offended but shortly afterwards the real culprit owned up, having been talking in class, and I was exonerated. In fact I was a painfully shy child. I think Ma imagined that her children would remain permanently biddable and she found it difficult to accept that we were developing personalities of our own. Once during my first year, I was walking with my much-loved father to the bus stop, and he asked me what was bothering me. I said: "I wish Mummy wouldn't nag me so." He didn't say much but when I returned home for lunch, I got an earful from Ma for complaining. My father had phoned home from the office. I learnt a very painful lesson that day: Throughout his life, Pa was a patient and gentle man but his loyalty, first and foremost, was always to Bessie, his wife. I never again complained to him about her. She really could be most difficult and argumentative and there were often scenes and tensions between her and Patrick and I which must have caused Pa great distress. Looking back, it is interesting to note that if either of us called out in the night when we were small, we always called for him, and he always came. This must have begun when we were babies, and he was protecting her from disturbed nights. I upset her more often than Patrick did – as a sickly child he needed a lot of care, and in any case he was the more phlegmatic. It is not surprising, looking back, that I was a bed-wetter for a number of years and this only caused more aggravation. Damp sheets would be draped over the banister, to my great embarrassment, to be replaced at night. Though I do wonder why I had a feather mattress on my bed!

During the Easter holidays of 1937, because I had had a lot of coughs and colds, I had my tonsils removed. I became very excited at this prospect, as the operation was to be done at home. I recall sliding about on the freshly-polished dining room table waiting for the doctor to come. By then our family doctor was a homeopath and a rather taciturn Scot. He brought a colleague to administer the anaesthetic and I was asked if I preferred lavender or eau-de-cologne. Never having heard of the latter, I opted for lavender. No doubt they were both ether. The next thing I remember is lying on the settee, feeling sore and being sick, and wondering why I had been so excited.

After a year in the Kindergarten we moved up to a form called Transition, where we were in the care of a nun called Sister Mary Immaculate. I'm afraid we called her Sister Mary Bad Tomato – she was a fierce and impatient lady, especially towards those children who seemed unable to master the basic principles of Arithmetic. I also suffered from the problem of being left-handed, and was forever having exercise books returned with the blots outlined in red and "untidy work" written in the margins. It was not a happy form. On one occasion I was threatened with being sent to Purgatory for some unremembered "crime" and on recounting this at home my mother immediately rang the Mother Superior demanding an explanation.

Patrick was not doing well at school having had chest problems and a lot of time off. One day when he was relatively well he went off with two of his friends to go fishing for tiddlers. The pond they chose was always afterwards known as "Typhoid Tarn" because he picked up typhoid fever and was seriously ill for weeks. He should have been sent to an Isolation Hospital but my feisty mother would have none of that, and she nursed him at home. For some time he was in an oxygen tent, and I had to be very quiet. When at last he was convalescing he was taught to knit, and he produced some fantastic dish cloths on the biggest needles available. He also loved to draw and paint. He was never a very intellectual child but he loved being read to. This was one of our mother's strengths and we both enjoyed listening to "The Inchcape Rock" and "How They Brought the Good News from Ghent to Aix" and any of the William books by Richmal Crompton.

The parents in Bournemouth, 1937.

Chapter 2
War Days

Those early days of September 1939 were glorious and for us, enjoying an extended holiday in Wales, peaceful and sunny. Pa had to return to work in Hull and had to drive alone, over the Pennines, to an empty house. He never did enjoy driving. In those halcyon days, we had a maid called Peggy, who came most days, and between them they had to rig up blackout curtains over all the windows, the house being typical of the age – all glass and concrete. When Ma later saw what they had done, the curtains all had to come down and be put up again "properly".

We had an extra 2 weeks in Wales and became more familiar with village life. The privy was at the end of the garden, surrounded by tall fuchsias, and we were there on the occasion that it was emptied at night. The village was really only a hamlet but there were 2 ladies called Jones. One was always addressed as Mrs Jones but the other, having a swarthy complexion, was always called "Dirty Mrs Jones". It sounded even worse in a Welsh accent and caused us a lot of amusement – I had learnt a little mimicry from Pa.

In mid-September, we returned to Hull by train and so back to school. The sky soon became thick with barrage balloons but little else happened until 1940, when the cold war abruptly ended. We became quite good at recognising aircraft and we learnt Morse Code. My dear peace-loving father decided that we should all learn to shoot and bought an airgun. We would take it in turns to have a pot at rabbits in the back garden but my mother was the only one to become proficient. When the bombing started, aimed at the docks, it was frightening to see the searchlights, hear the planes and the whining as the bombs came down, and then see the explosions all over dock area. The sky became an inferno, and the bombing always took place at night. We had a primitive air-raid shelter but our well-heeled neighbours had a very superior one, with electricity and bunks, and just occasionally, they would invite us to join them. But after a while, we decided that we would rather stay in our beds and face the possible consequences.

One day, after a particularly bad raid, Ma drove me the few miles into Hull to the Convent but all we could see was a smoking pile of rubble where my school had been. After a few days, it was decided that I should continue my education at Endsleigh Convent, where many of the nuns had gone, but it was the far side of Hull, and involved a journey of 2 buses. As the war continued unabated, after several weeks I was moved to the local school – Hessle Church of England. The contrast was great – discipline was much more lax and the children came from all sorts of backgrounds. We were visited once a term by the "nit nurse" and several children always had to be sent home for treatment. By this time, I had progressed from a fringe to plaits and dreaded having to undo them in school and then re-plait them after the tooth-combing. The school was only a mile from home, so I could now cycle to and from – good exercise as we had to go home for lunch. And heaven help us if we ever arrived at school without our gas masks. (To my great disappointment, I was considered too big to have a Mickey Mouse one).

Patrick had started at Beverley Grammar School for Boys on our return from Wales and he travelled to Beverley by bus every day. In 1941, when the war situation remained the same, it was decided that I too should go to Beverley, to the High School for Girls. So having passed the entrance examination, I started commuting too but not with Patrick. He preferred not to be seen with his little sister. Even in those days, the behaviour on buses was pretty dreadful, with a great deal of shoving, pushing, shouting and general ribaldry – from the boys! Once, I was standing on the running board on the way home, waiting to get off, when I was accidentally pushed off the bus. I hit my head on a lamp-post and lay unconscious for quite a while. Fortunately, Patrick was on the following bus and was very shocked to see me lying on the pavement with a crowd of onlookers. Somehow, he got me to my feet and walked me the mile up the hill home. I was taken down to the doctor in Hull to be stitched up and I was able to use "brain damage" as an excuse for quite a while. In fact, I was often in the wars, being a tomboy. Following a traffic accident when I was 5, I had to have "loops" in my lip; after the bus incident I had to be stitched on the back of my head; and later, there was an occasion when a friend and I were larking about on a haystack and thought it would be fun to slide down it together on to a cart. That caused a very bloody mess on my chin and the top of her head and we both had to be sutured. I was also prone to falling out of trees and scraping my knees in the playground. Sometimes, Patrick would tolerate my company and we had good fun tearing round the countryside on bikes, inspecting bomb craters and searching for shrapnel. I was very jealous of his ability to pee while cycling – and he didn't always warn me if I was behind.

As the war continued, Pa went to work every day by bus (he worked at a tar distillery and so was in a reserved occupation) but he often had to return at night for fire-watching duties. More than once, he just missed being hit by shrapnel. To help the war effort, he joined the Home Guard and took his duties very seriously. He always refused promotion, preferring to stay quietly in the background. My mother, ever resourceful, decided to keep chickens and ducks so that she could use the eggs for bartering and wheedling goods in short supply from "under the counter". My contribution to the war effort involved cleaning out the hen-house every Saturday morning and, for a short while, collecting nettles. These were tied up in great bundles and hung up in the kitchen to dry, when they were despatched for money. The proceeds were not worth the stinging effort.

Despite the war, we had some family holidays away and once stayed at a farm in the North Riding. We had a break from the bombing and we had an insight into farm life. Patrick and I "helped" with the threshing, with the men gradually working towards the middle of a large field where countless rabbits, mice and rats were trying to hide. The slaughter was great as they were hit on the head by the farm workers while trying to escape and the farm cats and dogs had a bonanza.

About this time (1941-2), serious thought was given to sending us to Canada "for the duration". Patrick and I were all for it but the idea was finally vetoed. And also about this time Ma became pregnant again and this may have been the deciding factor. She developed toxaemia, really because there was no ante-natal care then, and she became critically ill. She described, years later, how she had lost her sight and though she could feel the gas fire in their bedroom, she could not see it. When she was around 7 months pregnant and deteriorating, the doctor gave my father a syringe and some ampoules of Pitocin with which to induce

Pa, 1942

labour. It must have been almost impossible for him to do, because he was as soft as butter, and would not even kill a fly if he could help it, but it worked. Some hours later, my little sister was born prematurely and lived for just a few hours. We then had a living-in nurse, to care for Ma, but she was a most formidable lady. We were all terrified of her and were greatly relieved when it was decided that we could manage without her. She would throw her shoes into the kitchen for Pa to clean and shout out her order for lunch. Ma slowly recovered but it took her a long time to feel herself again.

We managed to have some treats, despite the wartime restrictions. We went to the pantomime in Leeds at Christmas-time by train and every Saturday, when Pa returned from work at lunch-time, we would discover that the "Fairy Postman" had been as there were 2 little bars of chocolate in our toy cupboard. Where Pa got chocolate from, I can't imagine, but the treat continued until Patrick became exasperated and announced that there was no such person as a "Fairy Postman". He was told that if the Fairy Postman heard him, he would not come again, and he never did. It was much the same at Christmas. We shared a bed on Christmas Eve so that Father Christmas would only have to visit one bedroom. We put our pillowcases at the foot of the bed and then he made me tie a piece of string to my big toe, with the other end on the door handle, so that I could wake him when "Father Christmas" came in and he could then be identified. We had overlooked the fact that the door opened inwards! The following year, Patrick went one better and having flattened a very large piece of Plasticine, put it by the door to get a footprint. Father Christmas must have seen the trap because he missed it but he never came again. So much for a brother!

Sometimes at weekends, if we had done all our homework, we would play games. We all enjoyed Monopoly but Patrick always insisted on being "banker". He always cheated, by hiding large sums of money between the leaves of the table, but when found out, he would, as he put it, "laugh till tears". Ma joined a Bridge school in about 1942 and when going off in the evening to play, would abjure my father to make sure that we went to bed on time. He was an innocent abroad in many ways, because we invented an "everlasting game" of cards and when bedtime was announced, we would say: "Can we just finish this game?" It was quite a while before we were rumbled.

Ma did not encourage us to have friends, or at least, invite them to the house. On the rare occasions when we did, they were severely criticised by Ma after they had gone. Pa's friends were treated similarly, so he arranged to meet them during the day. It was always embarrassing when, rarely, business friends came to stay, as despite her excellent cooking, Ma had no small talk and could never indulge in social chit-chat. Many years later, when Patrick and I were adults, we discovered that we not only had relatives, including a cousin a little younger than me, but that they lived just a couple of miles away. It transpired that Ma had fallen out with Pa's brother George and his fiancée before they were married and would thereafter have nothing to do with them. Some barriers were eventually broken down, after nearly 40 years, but relationships were never easy. Pa used to meet his brother in town from time to time, for lunch, and never let on, but the situation must have caused him a great deal of unhappiness as he was not used to deceit. He also had cousins who lived in Duffield, near Derby, and was particularly fond of Edna. They shared the same sense of the ridiculous and on the rare occasions when they phoned, there was a great deal of giggling, which upset Ma. I think that she was jealous of this relationship and certainly never encouraged it. She herself had a number of relatives but she seemed to have fallen out with them long ago. She was an only child, of ill-matched elderly parents, but she did have aunts, mostly schoolteachers, and presumably a few cousins. She was not, normally, a very warm person and we lacked cuddles and laughter from her in childhood. She did have a sense of humour but it was usually at someone's expense. She loved an argument and could not readily let matters drop – she was always right.

On the credit side, she was an excellent cook, albeit a very untidy worker. Her pastry was a light as a feather and her bread mouth-watering but the kitchen would usually be smothered in a dusting of flour. She took a passionate interest in gardening and in later years would open the garden to the public, for good causes, on 2 or 3 Sundays a year. She was also very artistic, painting usually in oils, and although she excelled at seascapes, she also tried portraiture, cats and flowers. One summer, she created a distant view of an Italian coastline seen through a balustrade, on a garden wall, and on another occasion, painted a very effective optical illusion of an arch and distant view on another wall. Her inventiveness was legendary. When the kitchen clock broke, she rescued the hands, found a china plate with the correct number of divisions in the pattern, drilled a hole in the middle, attached the hands, fixed a battery behind and hung the plate on the wall. On one occasion,

I arrived home for a few days' break and heard the cake-mixer going for the traditional welcome-home chocolate cake. In the kitchen, I saw the mixer mixing but no mother. She was down the garden picking peas for dinner! She had suspended the mixer by string from a cupboard handle into the mixing bowl which was revolving slowly on a round breadboard.

My mother was an amazing and multi-talented lady but never an easy one. She had been a pretty young woman and implied once that Pa had been lucky to catch her, but she had perversity in her make-up from childhood. As she advanced in years, she became increasingly difficult and criticised and alienated most of her friends. This was a great pity, as she had so much to offer, but as children we were often frightened of her and by her. She was always ready to slap and took my leather Brownie belt to my bare behind more than once. She could, in later years, be diverted by the suggestion of a game of Scrabble, at which she was expert, even if she did have her own rules and cheat by picking out the letters she wanted – if she thought nobody was looking.

My father, on the other hand, was so very different, being gentle, full of fun, loving, a great giggler, a hater of scenes and always ready to see the best in any situation. He was an upright Christian gentleman and would like to have been ordained. I think he realised that his wife would not have been able to tolerate the necessary sacrifices, or take on the role of a Vicar's wife. He contented himself with sidesman's duties but he would have made an excellent priest. One of his greatest joys was when Patrick was ordained. He was very conscientious, and a caring father, but quite impractical. He would have had great difficulty changing a light bulb but he could cut the finest bread and butter I have ever seen. It was he who kept in touch with us, once we had left home, writing in impeccable copper-plate at least once a week. His letters were always newsy and amusing but they also carried gentle reminders about behaviour and consideration for others. He was fond of dogs but almost besotted by cats and even in old age he could never pass a cat in the street without bending down to greet it and stroke it. He was never happier than when sitting with a cat purring on his knee. But he was so upset if an animal ever had to be put down.

He was a great reader, especially of political and historical biographies. He took a particular interest in the life of William Wilberforce and other great reformers. He loved churches, finding it difficult to pass one by without exploring it. As children, we found this interest rather boring and only later realised just how magnificent, and neglected, so many of our churches are.

Chapter 3
Boarding School Days

In 1944, things changed. The war continued to rage. Patrick had gone to Pocklington, a minor public school near York, because sickness had caused him to fall behind at Beverley and now it was my turn. Pa saw an advertisement in the *Church Times* for vacancies in a girls' school in Somerset and asked for details. In consequence, in September, we went down to Somerset by car, having hoarded petrol coupons, so that I could be interviewed. We stayed in Taunton and it had been agreed that if I was accepted, I would start at school immediately, a few days in advance of the Michaelmas Term. The school was at St. Audries, at West Quantoxhead in a lovely setting at the foot of the Quantock Hills, just a short distance from the sea.

So the following day we went to the school and I was interviewed by the Misses Kathleen and Laura Townshend, the elderly joint headmistresses who had founded the school. I was an extremely shy 12-year-old and had very little to say. After my parents had been interviewed, I learnt that Miss Laura had told them that I would be like putty in their hands and I was accepted. The school was part of the Woodward Foundation and therefore had strong Anglican connections.

We returned to Taunton for the night and the following day they drove back to Hull, trusting me to find my way from the hotel to the station, take the train to Williton, and then walk the mile or so up the hill to my new school. It was lovely autumn day, the roads were quiet and the hedgerows were full of blackberries.

Things changed too for my parents. The house was suddenly quiet and my mother, ever active and always in a rush (and usually late), turned to voluntary work. She worked with the Hull Braves (a corruption of the original Victorian title of the Poor Brave Things – the members being mostly crippled children and young adults). She also joined the WVS as it was then, and took round Meals on Wheels in the back of the car. She became involved in the Scout Movement and as an ex-teacher was Akela to the Hessle Wolf Cubs for quite a while. She joined the Townswomens' Guild and took part in various theatrical productions and much later she joined the Samaritans in Hull, relaying horrifying stories of near-suicides, drunken brawling and overdoses to my shocked father. They both had to make considerable sacrifices to send us both away to school and Ma would remind me of this whenever my reports were disappointing.

I found it difficult to settle down at St. Audries. I didn't mind being away from home – that was quite a relief – but it became apparent that I was the only child from the north in a West Country school and I was teased about my accent. By the end of the first term I had learnt to say "barth" instead of the clipped "a", and then of course I was teased in Yorkshire about my "posh" pronunciation. We had a strange and wonderful collection of teachers. Being wartime, many had been brought out of retirement, one or two were straight from college, and we had an ex-nun who had "jumped over the wall". We also had a few loyal stalwarts who were excellent and experienced teachers, especially Miss McLaren who taught History, Miss Yandle who was our English teacher, the terrifying Miss Hyatt, known as Hypot, who taught us Elocution and Singing. Miss Kathleen Townshend taught us French, and Miss Laura, the Catechism.

The dormitories were very basic and because of the recent expansion of the school, all the new girls were given truckle beds to sleep on. They had a tendency to collapse in the middle of the night which was a great ice-breaker and caused a lot of giggling. The lavatories were Victorian and the washing areas primitive. The classrooms were equipped with ancient desks engraved by countless names inked in over the years. The food was adequate but unappealing, but it was still wartime.

We were required to write home every Sunday afternoon and a postcard every Tuesday. Once, I commented on the "freezing weather" and was summoned to Miss Laura's office to define "freezing". We realised then that all postcards were read by authority. On Sunday mornings, after Chapel, we had to learn the Collect for that Sunday, and we were not released for more pleasurable pastimes until we had recited it, word perfect, to the mistress in charge. It is no surprise that the term time Collects are still familiar to me today. Later, we had to learn the Catechism in its entirety, which took weeks. Only then could we be considered for Confirmation.

At the end of my first term, in December 1944, I travelled by train to Sheffield, where Pa met me. Bouncing along the platform, full of excitement and holding his hand, I asked: "Do you like Handel's Largo?", whereupon he nearly had a fit, thinking I had said lager. I had during that first term been introduced to classical music. It was good to be home and enjoy a comfortable bed, good food, coal fires, baths and the company of cats, but it was not too long before the old tensions began to creep back in. And then it was almost a relief to return to school for the Spring Term.

Back at school, we were required to join the Cadet Force of the St John's Ambulance Brigade, Guides being unavailable. We were led by Miss McCann, an enormous lady well over 6 feet tall, who was very intimidating, with a strong Northern Irish accent. We were taught to march and expected to work towards various proficiency badges. I was given a length of grey material, already cut out, so that I could make my uniform dress. My left-handed disability then came to the fore – nobody could teach a left-hander to sew and French seams were beyond me. Countless times, the seams had to be unpicked because I'd got the material the wrong way round and it slowly became frayed and blood-stained from my pin-pricked fingers. I finished, eventually, some 3 years later, by which time it no longer fitted me, and it was passed on to an unsuspecting new girl. Later, one of the few prizes I won was an "Improvement in Needlework Prize" – I suppose, for effort.

In class, I was good Spelling, fairly good at Mental Arithmetic, and I enjoyed English and History lessons, mainly because of the quality of the teaching. During French lessons, taken by Miss Kathleen, we all had to be on our best behaviour. Latin was taught by Miss Nicholson, who also taught Needlework, so she knew what she was up against with me. I could have enjoyed Latin but one winter's evening, as the sun was setting, she became totally exasperated with me and bringing down my Latin textbook firmly on my head, proclaimed that she could not teach me any more Latin. I pretended to take that as a compliment. I have always regretted having to give up Latin, but it was out of my hands. We used to chant:

Latin is a language as dead as dead can be,
It killed the ancient Romans, and now it's killing me.
All are dead who spoke it, all are dead who wrote it,
All are dead who learnt it – lucky dead! They earned it.

Slowly, my education progressed and I grew in height if not in wisdom. One term, we had a new teacher, brought out of retirement, to help with Geography. She was very short, and very round, and wore, apparently, countless layers of clothes. We did not like her very much and on one occasion we arranged several drawing pins, points uppermost, on the teacher's seat, to see if they would penetrate. She failed to react and later, after a boring lesson, went out with several pins stuck to her skirt. About the same time, when we were rebellious fourth formers, and aged around 14, the whole form was sent to Coventry and the mistresses refused to teach us. I can't recall what precipitated this dramatic event (the majority of us were not involved) but we had no lessons for several days. I don't think my poor father, paying the fees, ever got to hear of this incident. I hope not.

Some of us were very keen to learn "the facts of life" – we were all so green and innocent in those days. A smuggled-in magazine offered a booklet explaining things and we sent off for it. As we could not expect to have such material delivered to the school, we arranged to have it sent to the Post Office at the end of the drive to await collection. Two of us, after several days had passed, walked up the drive to the Post Office, which was out of bounds, to collect the packet .The old lady who kept the Post Office questioned us quite severely but we had thought of plausible reasons for our actions and she handed the packet over, declining to report us. The booklet became very dog-eared as it was passed around but it did not tell us a great deal. We learnt much more from some of the banned books which were smuggled in – "Forever Amber" springs to mind!

During 1946, the Misses Townshend retired and a new headmistress was appointed – Miss Cynthia Havergal. She was relatively young, very well qualified, and she brought a breath of fresh air into the school. In the spring of 1947, I was prepared for Confirmation and this event co-incided with the appalling weather which hit the country at that time. Snow persisted for weeks and some of the little local lanes were not only totally blocked, but we could walk along the top, level with the hedgerows, if we were suitably clad. Lynton and Lynmouth,

September 1945. Returning to school 1 year on. In winter school uniform.

At school in 1947 in the summer school uniform.

The "Management", 1947.

further down the coast, were hit by atrocious storms and suffered severe damage. And so it was, in March, with many of the major roads blocked and most of the rail network out of action, that Pa somehow came down from Hull for the day for my Confirmation. I will never know how he managed it and he must have been exhausted.

As I moved up the school, so the quality of dormitory improved, and as the war approached its end, many restrictions were lifted and the food and standard of teaching became a little better. I had piano lessons, for which I showed little aptitude, from a short and short-tempered mistress inappropriately called Miss Long. I had riding lessons and enjoyed some marvellous trips over the Quantocks on Saturday afternoons. In the summer, whatever the weather, we were allowed to go down in a "crocodile" to the beach at West Quantoxhead. But the beach was small and stony, and not conducive to swimming. I excelled at sport, especially athletics. I was usually the last leg in the relay and enjoyed high jumping. During my last year, some of us were entered for the Somerset Junior Athletic Championships in Taunton and came back with pride and certificates.

Towards the end of my schooldays, because of expansion, a few of us were allowed to move up to sleeping accommodation in the Rectory at the end of the drive. The Rector and his wife had no children and quite a lot of spare room, and we enjoyed being in a more normal environment. We had to cross a fairly busy road to reach the Rectory, so Miss Havergal approached the local authorities to see if a "School Crossing" sign could be erected. After much deliberation, presumably because of post-war restrictions, all they could offer was a sign reading "Cattle Crossing".

By 1948, my future had become a matter of urgent discussion. I had always wanted to be a teacher, either at Kindergarten level or Games. I would have been following in the footsteps of relatives on both sides of the family but it was pointed out that I would have to work a great deal harder to achieve that ambition. There was very little help available on careers advice and possible alternatives. The situation was not helped by my low self-esteem and not knowing what my strengths were. I worked as hard as I could before taking the Oxford School Certificate in the summer of 1948, and went home at the end of term to await the results. I failed, and gloom descended. Any thoughts I might have had of University or Teachers' Training College were ruled out and I was thoroughly in disgrace at home, having let the side down and wasted a great deal of money. The awful thing was that I had done well in English, History, French, and even Art but to get a Pass, one had to pass in Mathematics as well as English, and that was my weakest subject. After much heart-searching, it was decided that I would return to St. Audries for a further year; to retake the whole thing, instead of going on to take the Higher School Certificate. It was also decided for me that I should apply for nurse training, which did not appeal to me at all. To let me down lightly, it was suggested that I should try for Orthopaedic Nursing, which was thought to be less traumatic than general nursing. So during my last year, I applied to the Wingfield-Morris Orthopaedic Hospital in Oxford and was accepted, subject to my exam results.

I took the beastly exams again and in the summer of 1949 went home to again await the results. This time, although I had failed in Geometry, Algebra and Trigonometry, I had scraped a pass in Arithmetic. And because I had also improved my grades in the other subjects, I was awarded a "Compensated" Certificate. So I was able to enjoy some relief and a little freedom before starting training in December in Oxford.

Patrick, meanwhile, had left Pocklington and having worked briefly at a local farm, had gone to Agricultural College in Wales. He had not done very well either in examinations but as the years progressed, we were both able to show that we were not total dimwits. It is interesting to realise now how much depended on encouragement (which was lacking for me), standards of teaching. and the standard of public examinations. By modern standards, I would almost certainly have gone to University.

Chapter 4
Training Days

In December 1949, I reported to Pollock House in North Oxford, which was where the Preliminary Training School was held for the Wingfield-Morris Orthopaedic Hospital. There were 8 of us, all 17 or 18 years old, and all very apprehensive. Having travelled by train from Hull to Oxford, one of my concerns was my bike which had travelled down in the guards van. I had had to leave it at the station, being burdened with luggage. I discovered that Biddy McLean, a bubbly dark-haired Scot, had left her bike too, so the next day, with permission, we went down by bus and cycled back. Our first few days were spent getting to know each other and the staff of Pollock House. Our Sister Tutor was a very fierce red-haired lady called Sister Houghton, who stood no nonsense.

Our small group consisted of Mary Gibb, who had come from South Africa where her father was Dean of Cape Town; Jane Latham, as tall and thin as a beanpole; Anne Merriman, a vicar's daughter; Sally Cook, who was a little wild; Sheila Wilmott, a very sensible girl; Molly Freeman who was more untidy than me; and Biddy. We had lectures every morning and practical classes in the afternoons, and every week we had a written test. We learnt how to make a bed properly, how to "blanket bath" (using each other as very embarrassed "patients"), how a bedpan should be given (and removed) and how to prepare for countless procedures like enemas, hair-washing in bed and simple dressings.

The course lasted 8 weeks and at the end of the fourth, having had a brief break at home for Christmas, we were put into stiff, unyielding uniforms and taken up to the hospital and on to the wards for the first time. I don't think much was expected of us and they were not disappointed. We all returned to the safety of Pollock House absolutely shattered and appalled at what lay ahead of us. The pressures then began to build up, and faced with exams at the end of the course which would determine whether or not we continued our training, we had to get down to really hard work – revising, drawing bones and muscles, and asking each other questions. As a little light relief, we woke one morning to a white world. It had snowed really hard in the night and Mary, who had never seen snow before, rushed downstairs in her nightdress and out into the garden to feel snow on her face and her feet. I imagine the novelty wore off quite quickly.

During the last 3 weeks, we were taken up to the hospital for one afternoon session every week, always to the same ward, so that we began to familiarise ourselves with the staff and patients. During the last week, we took our exams, in anatomy, physiology and general nursing. Strangely, every morning, our Sister Tutor, of whom we had become fond, would come down to breakfast and relate another fantastic dream. We realised that she wanted us all to pass and was therefore giving us the broadest hints possible on the questions. One morning she told how she had dreamt of falling off a bus and fracturing her femur and on another, how she had dreamt of enjoying a meal of liver and onions. We had a short time to rush off and check on the structure of the femur and the physiology of the liver.

We all passed and after a weekend at home, returned to Oxford, this time going straight to the hospital. We all had rooms in the nurses' home, and initially depended on each other for support and comfort. On my first day, wandering round the corridors, I thought how strange it was that the name plates on the doors apparently showed everyone's name beginning with "N". I couldn't think of many names starting with N, except for Nancy and Nora, and then the penny dropped. Apart from our own small set, Christian names were not used. We were invariably addressed by our surnames, sometimes with "Nurse" in front, but often not.

And so to the wards, where much of our training went straight out of the window. I was asked to prepare for a blanket bath and spent ages trying to remember the 28 items which I had been taught were necessary. I was scolded for taking so long and the bare essentials were whipped off my beautiful trolley and rushed to the patient. It was all hard work and we had to learn to be quick making beds, sweeping the ward floors (having first sprinkled tea-leaves on them) rushing round meals and keeping things tidy. I was slow and clumsy and kept leaving fingers behind in swing doors and breaking thermometers. If one broke a thermometer, one had to take the pieces up to Matron's office and explain oneself. On my third visit in almost as many weeks, Miss Jolliffe, the Matron, showed me again, with great exasperation, how to shake a thermometer down correctly and promptly broke it on the side of her desk. It was difficult to keep a straight face.

Our shifts meant that we were on duty from 8.00 in the morning until 8.00 at night, with 3 hours off during the day – either from 10.00-1.00 or 2.00-5.00. Once a week, before a day off, we finished at 5.00. We had 1 day off a week and so worked about 50 hours a week. We earned around £10 per week but it was pointed out to us that this was all spending money as the uniform, board lodging and laundry were all provided. One of the first things I bought was a Bush wireless, to my father's horror, on the "never-never", but it was lovely on a day off to have breakfast brought to one in bed and listen to the programmes.

After 12 weeks, we all changed wards and had to start all over again getting to know the staff and patients. I moved from a women's ward to a children's ward. All the patients had orthopaedic conditions, often resulting from TB or Polio, and many were there for a very long time, some in plaster beds, some in traction and others in plaster jackets. Many had surgery to correct deforming conditions. We were expected to know the full name, age, religion, diagnosis and treatment of all the patients on a ward on the day we arrived there. When Matron did her rounds before lunch every day, it often fell to the lot of one of the Junior Probationers to accompany her. Some of the patients, especially the men, were very naughty, and no doubt bored, and would do their best to confuse us about their treatment, causing us great confusion until we got wise to them.

As our training continued, we moved every 12 weeks from one ward or department to another, including the plaster room, the theatres, where the senior staff waited in eager anticipation for a junior to faint while watching their first amputation of the leg, and the private wing. The children's wards were awful, as the long term children were very difficult to control. They would throw food around, hide illicit magazines and sweets under their mattresses, and give new nurses a great deal of lip. My education broadened. After 6 months I went on night duty for the first time and my education broadened even more from randy men confined to bed for long periods. We got to know the

With Patrick, 1950

Preliminary Training School Wingfield-Morris Orthopaedic Hospital, Oxford, January 1950. Author middle back

patients very well as they were hospitalised for so long, and we got to know them best at night when the adults particularly wanted to talk.

At the end of our first year, we took the State Preliminary examination. We had to pass it before continuing further. This meant several written papers, practical tests, and worst of all, a *viva voce* with one of the Consultants. This meant sitting down with one of these revered gentlemen and being confronted with an array of bones, instruments and pieces of medical equipment. He would pick up an item and pass it to the victim, who had to describe everything they knew about it. With bones, it was not just the anatomical features that were required but also the names and insertions of muscles and ligaments, and possible abnormalities and treatment. They must have had a job keeping straight faces sometimes. I told the examiner once, in a state of terror, everything about the humerus he had passed me. After several minutes, he looked at me, probably saw my trembling fingers, and said: "You don't really mean all that, do you?" Then I realised that I was holding and describing a femur. He was a gentleman. I passed.

More wards and more night duty followed and we slowly became more confident and were given more responsibility as more groups started their training below us. As we approached the end of our training, decisions had to be made. Some of our set never completed their training, finding the stresses too much, but most of us decided to train further. Having embarked on this profession, to which I was never really suited, I thought that I might as well try to make the best of it, so I applied to most of the top London hospitals for general training. My parents must have been very relieved that I was sticking to nursing and in time they became proud of me, but they never knew my real feelings.

In my last few months in Oxford, I went up to London and was interviewed by the Matron of St. Thomas's Hospital. Greatly to my surprise, I was accepted for general training, subject to passing my final orthopaedic examinations. I was surprised because I had heard that one was only accepted if one's family was well-connected. We later discovered that those with previous training had a better chance of being accepted.

Back in Oxford, we took our exams, both hospital and state, and having passed, we had several months when we were superfluous Senior Probationers but we had to fill in time until we could move on. The early summer of 1952 was glorious and we joined the crowds

Pa, 1950.

celebrating May Day by cycling down to Magdalen Bridge before it was fully light to hear the choirboys singing from the top of the tower. We had made the most of our time in Oxford, having learnt to punt, and joined in a few of the undergraduate "goings-on". My parents took me abroad for the first time and we went, by train, to Kitzbuhel, for 2 weeks in the early summer surrounded by meadows full of flowers and distant snow-capped mountains. We took a trip up the Gross Glockner by charabanc and saw Hitler's alpine hideout.

Back in England, before starting my general training in June 1952, I was told to report to the Manor House in Godalming, in Surrey, for another Preliminary Training School. The PTS was held here because it was fairly near the branch hospital of St. Thomas's at Hydestile. This hospital was hutted and had been established during the war as a refuge from the main hospital, and was a pleasant and gentle introduction. The lovely summer weather continued and at Manor House we joined a large group of girls who were mostly straight from school. They were very well-spoken, some had cars, but they were all terrified. There were 8 of us in our "short set", having undertaken a previous training, and although we were apprehensive, we did have some idea of what lay in store. The lectures and demonstrations were all carried out with extreme professionalism – there were no Sister Tutors here having helpful little dreams the night before exams.

We were taken up to the wards at Hydestile in small groups to sample ward work. I was allocated to a male surgical ward, and because not a great deal was expected of me, I was able to keep a low profile. By September, most of us having completed the course, we moved to the nurses' home at Hydestile for several weeks before going up to London. The atmosphere was very relaxed and friendly and we had a delightfully eccentric Home Sister called Miss Drummond-Hay. On one occasion I noticed that her spectacles, which had been tied up with string and Selotape, had been replaced by new ones. When I commented, she said: "Yes. I found them in someone's waste-paper basket!" She was responsible for the welfare and discipline of the student nurses. Once, one of the Senior Probationers with a title flew over to Paris to buy a hat for a wedding. Unfortunately, her return was delayed by fog, and so she was late on duty. The next day, Home Sister put up a notice reading: NURSES MUST NOT GO ABROAD ON THEIR DAYS OFF! That same offender, some time later, bought a little black Morris and called it Malaena. The patients all thought it was such a pretty name for a car, unaware that in medical parlance it meant blood in the stools. Many years later, Miss Drummond-Hay was found to have quietly died in the corner of a first class railway carriage returning to London from Scotland.

And so to London. We all went up in a group, quaking in our highly-polished shoes and bearing a perfectly-made cap. Mine had been made for me by someone with nimbler and less clumsy fingers than mine. Our caps were very difficult to make; having been starched and pressed with a gophering iron, we had to sew milliner's wire into them and force the pleats into an acceptable shape. The main problem was that if one had a good one, one tended to hang on to it for far too long, until the grime of London made it untenable. On arrival, we were given rooms in Gassiot House, which overlooked the Thames and the Houses of Parliament, and having found our bearings, settled in. The following morning, we all arrived at our respective wards, feeling very conspicuous and apprehensive. I was sent to a female surgical ward where, to my great relief, the Ward Sister was kind and patient. I was let down lightly. Our duties, initially, were basic cleaning – the bedpans, the lockers and the long red mackintoshes which were automatically made into each bed. They had to be scrubbed and many of them were very old and cracked. They must have been so uncomfortable. I was also allowed to assist with bedpan rounds and emptying sputum mugs – to me, the worst possible job which really made me heave. Bedmaking was relatively straightforward but it had to be done properly, with the bedding folded correctly, all corners mitred when put back; the sheet had to have a turnover of precisely 18 inches (one Sister, subsequently, carried a ruler with her!) and the counterpane had to be so positioned that the hospital crest was absolutely dead-centre. The bedding was then eased over the feet for movement and the pillows arranged for maximum comfort. Finally, the wheels were turned in so that nobody could trip over them.

Our lives on the wards were governed by Big Ben. The early shift started at 7.30, Sister would arrive at 7.40, and we would all follow her in to her office to hear the night report. We could not, of course, sit there with idle hands, and on each chair some "work" had been placed, which was either folding gauze or making swabs to very particular criteria. And while we were busy, we listened and remembered. If the report was quick, we continued to sit, in silence but still working, until the first notes of Big Ben sounded. Sister would rise, sweep into the suddenly-hushed ward, and descend gracefully to her knees for morning prayers as the sound of the last stroke faded away.

The wards were long "Nightingale" wards, with 15 beds down each side, and sometimes, if there had been a number of emergencies, down the middle as well. Then, no patient would have been turned away because of a bed shortage. Also down the middle were Sister's desk, cupboards called "ambulances" holding equipment and lotions and a steriliser, and incredibly, now, an open fire! For procedures and dressings we used heavy china "porringers" – small round ones for lotions, large round ones for dressings and rectangular ones for instruments. These all had to be boiled in the steriliser, along with catheters and other rubber items. Heaven help you if you forgot, or were too busy to go back after 5 minutes! The smell of "catheter jam" gave you away and lingered for hours.

This, to me as a new Junior Probationer, was all in the future. I had only been on the ward for a few weeks when the Ward Sister was moved and a veritable dragon arrived. She was a very impatient lady. We had eye patients at the far end of the ward, and in those days they were double-padded and had to lie motionless for 10 days to allow their surgery to heal, in an atmosphere of peace and quiet. One day, a hapless colleague dropped a tray of full teacups at that end and the noise was dreadful. Sister came storming down the ward, which became very hushed, and the tirade began. We had heard that she was shortly to be married and when at last she stopped, an elderly patient said: "Well, Sister, I hope you are going to be kinder to your husband than you are to these poor nurses!"

If we were on a "split shift", we went off duty at 2.00 but only if we could present to Sister the correct number of clean and folded cloths with which we had been working. We came back at 5.00, and then worked until 8.00, when evening prayers were said by the Senior Nurse. The sight of that person advancing down the ward holding a hassock and prayer card was enough to send the visitors scurrying home.

Sometimes, we were "off duty" from 10.00 until 1.00, but this was not popular as we were still involved in the heavy morning cleaning. It just gave one time to nip into the West End by bus (the conductors invariably let us travel free but we then had to listen sympathetically to their ailments). At that time, there was a delightful café in Regent Street called the Chocolate House, where one could have different sorts of chocolate drinks to the accompaniment of Mozart, which was always being played in the background.

So that was the pattern of our lives as Student Nurses. Every 3 months, we moved to a new ward to vary our experience and always before leaving the old one, we had to ask Sister to complete our "schedule". This was a very comprehensive chart of all the procedures to be learnt. Sister put a stroke if we had been shown how to do something, and a cross if, after questioning, we were thought to be proficient. This list included everything, from simple dressings to suture removal, from "tooth-combing" (still at that time a routine procedure on admission) to last offices.

I commenced my general training in the summer of 1952 and in November of that year, we had the last Great Smog. It was alarming, in that one could not see one end of the ward from another, and we were inundated with patients with acute breathing problems. Because we were young and fit, at times the situation became something of an adventure. By then I was living in a nurses' home on the Chelsea Embankment and we were normally transported by hospital coach. Because of the smog, no traffic was running, the streets were deserted and eerily quiet. After coming off duty one evening, a number of us decided to attempt the journey to Chelsea. Although the authorities tried to dissuade us, we walked over Westminster Bridge, groping our way not being able to see more than a yard in front. Suddenly, Big Ben above us boomed the hour and we nearly jumped into the river in fright. We found the tube station and found the trains were running, and so went to Sloane Square, our nearest stop. This was still a good 10-minute walk and the smog here was as thick as ever. We were regretting our foolishness when we were met by 2 policemen with flares and they escorted us all the way back. When I finally reached my room, a clean sheet and pillowcase had been left on my bed for changing and when I picked up the pillowcase, a dirty brown rectangle remained on the sheet below. And the window was closed.

1952 was still a time of rationing. When I had 2 nights off after 10 on, if I was going away, I was given little twists of tea and sugar, an ounce each of butter and cheese, and 2 rashers of bacon to give to whoever I planned to stay with. Night duty in a busy hospital was a pretty frightening experience, as we were always extremely busy, and the time flew by on a 12-hour shift. Most of us found it difficult to sleep during the day and at the end of 3 months, we were absolutely shattered.

There was usually a study block after night duty, which let us down gradually, and prepared us for more responsibility. Those of us with a previous training were doing our general training in 3 years instead of 4, so with every study block we "leap-frogged" and joined another group. Although we got to know more people, we never really felt as though we belonged to one set.

Towards the end of my training, I was sent to the Waterloo Hospital, which had become part of the group. It was very old-fashioned and quaint and catered mostly for children having their tonsils and adenoids out, patients with hernias and varicose veins, and psychiatric patients. This was, in fact, a crafty move on my part. I had been allocated to a ward of chest patients, with a Sister with whom I had crossed swords on night duty, and I knew it wouldn't work. So I went to Matron's office and pointed out that I was nearing the end of my training and I had had no theatre experience! So to the Waterloo I went, and spent 4 months there, gaining theatre experience as well as an insight into the treatment of psychiatric patients. All of them had to be checked every 15 minutes, night and day, and I did not enjoy helping with the treatments.

The main hospital was about half a mile away and I had to return there to take first my hospital finals, for which I had to produce a many-tailed bandage, sewn with red blanket stitch. Not easy for the left-hander! The hospital exam consisted of written papers and a practical part, and the latter was in fact worse than the State equivalent as our examiners were formidable and familiar Senior Sisters. Our written papers were marked by the Consultants, who then examined us orally. In all, a terrifying business. The State Final examinations were a little easier in that we did not know our inquisitors. We were fortunate in that the State Practical was held at St. Thomas's (not always the case) so the equipment was familiar. At other times, finalists had been sent to other hospitals and were lost in that our "porringers" were unique to us.

At last, it was all behind us, bar the waiting. When the results were posted up in Matron's office, we all tore down and then could not bear to look, in case we had failed. Those of us who had passed, and we were in the majority, could not celebrate because some of our friends had failed. Words of comfort were quite inadequate.

I had decided to do my midwifery training and had applied to, and been accepted by, the Sorrento Maternity Hospital in Birmingham. Before I left St. Thomas's, where I had not really been happy in such a large institution, I was extremely surprised to be asked by Matron if I would like to return as a Charge Nurse (the modern equivalent being a Staff Nurse), and I was so shocked that I accepted. I thought at the time that this was great honour but later learnt that to be asked to return was common practice!

I had a short break at home and then, in the autumn of 1955, arrived at the Sorrento with a friend of mine from London. I was glad that Ann Baron was with me, as we discovered quite quickly that there was a great deal of resentment among all grades of staff towards London-trained Pupil Midwives. It soon became less of a problem, because both Ann and I had done a previous training and were therefore not quite as green and inexperienced as some.

Chapter 5
Gaining Experience

In 1955, conditions for expectant and nursing midwives, and for Pupil Midwives, left a great deal to be desired. As learners, we were not entitled to a room of our own, but had to share. Night duty came round quite frequently and we were expected to attend lectures in the middle of the day – our night, as far as sleeping went. We would be summoned at all hours to witness a delivery, especially if it was an unusual one. But the first delivery I saw was an unforgettable and very moving experience. I don't think a good midwife ever ceases to identify and empathise with a woman in labour, and I knew that I would enjoy this aspect of nursing.

The Sorrento Maternity Hospital had outgrown its original premises years previously and several local properties had been acquired for expansion, including 2 semi-detached houses. These were connected to the main part of the hospital where all the deliveries took place, by passing through gardens and across grounds. This was not much fun for a lady in strong labour, or indeed for a just-delivered mother, especially as the journey, on a trolley, was nearly all outside and over rough and uneven paths. We were there during a very hard and snowy winter. Having got a new mother and her baby safely into one of the houses, we then had to negotiate the trolley round the bends in the staircase to the waiting bed upstairs. But we were young and fit, and in any case, had no choice.

We had to witness a specific number of normal deliveries before being allowed to deliver ourselves – under close supervision. We also had to see as many abnormal deliveries as possible – apart from forceps and breech deliveries, there were Caesarean Sections, multiple births and infants with malpresentations, abnormalities and stillbirths. These were always upsetting for everyone but became a little more acceptable if the baby had gross deformities. One of the Consultants was a lady of international repute and we were summoned on one occasion to watch her delivering a breech. The mother was in the customary very inelegant position, with her legs slung up to give a clear field, and one tiny foot was visible. The consultant impressed on us all the need for patience, as the rest of the baby started slowly to appear, with gravity and contractions. The consultant sat on a stool very close to the field of activity, with a bucket at her feet to catch some of the inevitable mess, and while she was explaining a point to us, the baby dropped straight into the bucket. As we all wore masks in those days, our facial expressions were invisible, including those of the very embarrassed consultant. The bawling baby suffered no ill effects.

The time came for me to deliver my first baby. The first stage of labour was usually spent in one of the wards off the delivery suite and the mother only moved when she was in the second stage. Fortunately, my first patient had had a previous baby and everything was straightforward, quick and easy. But I can still recall the feeling of a kind of miracle as the infant, briefly a lifeless mass of pale flesh, took a breath, cried, and became pink and active. I found it very moving.

The 6 months of training proceeded and I became more efficient and confident. Having taking the Part 1 exams, most of us were considering our next steps. I realised that I wanted very much to qualify as a midwife but first I had to honour the agreement I had with St. Thomas's and return as a Charge Nurse.

So I returned to London, to work at the Grosvenor Hospital in Vincent Square, which was the base for the gynaecological unit. I had been appointed to work on the 1st Floor, as Deputy to Miss Elliott. Arriving on my first morning, I felt very self-conscious in my blue long-sleeved uniform and wondered if I was doing the right thing. However, Miss Elliott, although she could be fearsome, was kind to me and gave me some much-needed self-confidence. She was a hard taskmaster and I had to remember all I was told – note-taking was not allowed.

The Grosvenor was a strange hospital, converted from a private dwelling. It had a lift but it was so small that patients going to and from theatre on the 3rd Floor had to travel on a very short trolley with their knees bent up. On the 1st Floor, we had 24 beds, all in wards of 4 or 6, but one ward was up 10 steps, which meant that we had to carry post-operative patients up to their beds. If there was a death, which happened fairly frequently, the body had to be taken down in the lift as soon as possible, again with knees bent, so that the body could be "laid out" on the ground floor. Later on, to reach the mortuary, we had to wait until the coast was clear of visitors and then, having placed the body on a standard trolley, we pushed it along a short corridor, take a right-angled turn to the left and continue along another short corridor which ended with a door to the extreme left. However, there was a small window facing and because the angle to the door was too sharp to get the trolley through, we had first to open the window, push the body halfway through and balance it while another nurse squeezed through the door and balanced the body from the other side. The first person then brought another trolley from the mortuary across the yard, the body was safely moved on to it, and so to the peace of the mortuary. Stifled giggles were inevitable, and there was always great relief when the job was done. There never seemed to be any porters around to help.

Once a year, an inventory was held of all the linen on the premises. We seemed to be perpetually short of sheets, draw sheets and pillowcases, despite them being counted out and counted back. The Matron of the Grosvenor was very like a character on the radio at that time called Mrs Feather – she twittered and got nowhere fast. I don't think she ever realised how we deceived her over the linen. Each ward and department had its own lists and it was a matter of pride that we should be seen to be short, but not *too* short, so that further supplies could be justified. If "Mrs Feather" started her check at the top of the building, those numbers would have been made more or less correct by loans from the floors below by using the back stairs and surreptitious refolding of items. We were usually given a hint as to where she would start by her sympathetic secretary. If she started at the bottom of the building, the plan was reversed. This checking of the inventory was a very serious business and I don't think she ever realised that her "girls", all in connivance, were tearing up and down the back stairs with piles of linen.

Bearing in mind that it was now 1957, it is difficult to believe that we had coal-burning fires in all our wards at the Grosvenor and very comforting they were too to our ill patients. Some had been prescribed long warm soaks to aid healing, so they were put in a hip bath in front of the fire, decently screened off from prying eyes. And we had yellow plastic ducks! Then, patients would stay for several weeks, and one got to know them really well. Today's nurses are not really able to build up much of a relationship with their patients, as they stay in hospital for such a short time. We worked hard, for long hours, but our patients were happy, and by and large, so were we. Money could not be given to individual nurses but we were never short of chocolates, and sometimes gifts became imaginative and personal, like stockings or slips. One lady who I came to know well, invited me to the theatre following her discharge and we saw "At the Drop of a Hat" with Michael Flanders and Donald Swann. On another occasion, I was invited to dinner with a lady who had been the Headmistress of a girls' school in Nairobi. Not only did I enjoy an excellent meal but also I was introduced to Scrabble, which I seem to have been playing ever since.

I worked, and lived, at the Grosvenor for 18 months and towards the end of it, I had been planning my next move. I wanted to qualify as a Midwife but because I had had a break in training, I was required to undergo a 6-week refresher course. So I left the Grosvenor and went to the maternity unit of the main hospital for 6 weeks. Then I moved to Camberwell to undertake our final 6 months of training, with 7 others, "on the district". We were attached to the General Lying-In Hospital, also part of the St. Thomas's group, but we had opted for training entirely on the district.

The house in Camberwell was the base for us and a resident Staff Midwife. We also had a cook and a cleaner but otherwise we had to look after ourselves. We had to be able to ride a bike and answer the switchboard (something I never mastered!). We took it in turns to take calls, night and day, and if it was one of our own patients, we then had to proceed, with all the necessary equipment, to the given address, on our bikes, where we would be joined either by the Staff Midwife or the Midwife in charge of us. This lady did not live with us and having failed her driving test, and being unable to ride a bike, used to walk everywhere, very fast. She was a fairly terrifying lady, with little patience with us learners, and we would wait in a degree of apprehension for the little feet clattering down the street. We had to become familiar, very quickly, with the geography of the area we covered, which was mostly in Bermondsey and Camberwell.

The first case I was called to, I found fairly quickly. The mother lived in very poor circumstances, in a flat with 3 other children, all of whom were bedwetters. The smell was quite something and the children all ran around wearing nothing but vests. I arrived about lunchtime (the Midwife shortly afterwards) to find that the mother was in established labour but all she had for the new arrival were 2 little jackets knitted from angora wool. The father was nowhere to be seen and it transpired that he was currently in prison. The family was well known to the Midwife. On his spells at home, in between sentences, the father made and sold toffee apples, which were stored, uncovered, under the only bed. I had to learn, very fast, how to improvise because the new baby arrived soon after we did. Once labour was over satisfactorily, the Midwife went tittuping on her way, leaving me to do all the clearing up and writing up the records. There was something immensely satisfying, even in this poor situation, of cycling back with a job well done. On our return, we had to restock our bags immediately in case we were called out to another case. We were individually responsible for the ongoing care of all those patients we had delivered, which meant visiting them daily, making sure that there were no problems with mother or baby, and helping to establish breast-feeding. After 14 days, the responsibility passed to the local Health Visitor.

Six months on the district passed by very quickly, despite constant problems with punctures to our bikes. We became adept at record-keeping and maintaining our equipment, which consisted of a large midwives' bag, and a portable gas and air machine. It was a hectic time but very satisfying, and I have happy memories – a red-headed mother who delivered ginger twins and managed to feed them simultaneously, and cycling downhill on Christmas morning, where every home I visited insisted on "lacing" the inevitable cup of tea. I learnt to judge a home by the milk bottles outside – mostly, in that part of London, they had sterilised milk, which was disgusting in tea. I felt in clover on the rare occasions I saw a pasteurised bottle. I have never liked strong tea but I learnt to drink it on the district, despite the state of some of the cups and mugs I was offered. The atmosphere in Bermondsey at that time was marvellous – a nurse on a bike could go anywhere safely and was greeted cheerfully by everyone.

And then with the final exams looming, it was decision time again. I applied to the P&O shipping line and to Princess Mary's RAF Nursing Service among others, and was interviewed and offered posts by both. There seemed to be a lot of "dressing up" on board ship, so I went for the PMRAFNS, subject to qualifying as a Midwife and passing a medical examination. Right at the end of our 6 months on the District,

2 of us went down with flu. We got no sympathy from the Midwife who said that the trouble with young people was that they had no stamina. It meant that we had to make up 2 weeks after we had taken the exams and we would have to do it at the General Lying-In Hospital, as a new batch of Pupil Midwives was moving in. So June and I reported to the GLI as soon as we were fit. The 2 weeks passed very quickly but one incident remains fresh in my mind. Incredibly now, at that time post-natal mothers were kept in bed for 10 days, and on the 10th day they were "churched". This involved them attending a service to give thanks for a safe delivery. There was still a superstition in 1958 in that part of London at least that no woman could appear in public until she had been churched, as until then she was regarded as unclean.

So one morning, I was asked to take a group of mothers down one floor in the lift to the chapel for the service. The lift was very large and very old with cage doors at the front and the back, and it had an official capacity of 12 persons. I had forgotten this limit and herded the ladies into the lift and pressed the button to go down. The lift moved a few feet, juddered, and stopped. We were stuck between floors. I pressed the emergency button and suggested that the ladies sat on the floor. After a few minutes, the Matron's head appeared, gazing up from the floor below. "How many patients have you got in there Nurse?" she asked. "Er, I think there are 14," I said, having by now read the notice. "Can't you count?" came the acid question. At that moment, the head of the Deputy Matron appeared at the door at the other end, also gazing up, and she then started questioning me. I slowly built up the numbers, appearing to be exceedingly stupid and unable to count. They had to send to St. Thomas's over the road for an engineer to wind the lift down and when we finally emerged on the floor below, Matron was counting heads on one side and her Deputy on the other. I had had 20 patients in the lift, and received a very severe and justified reprimand. The mothers were none the worse and having by then missed the service, were escorted back up the stairs. They could not really punish me, as I was supernumerary and leaving 2 days later in any case.

Having then completed my third training, I went home to Hull for a short break and to await the results. During this time, I worked briefly at the local maternity hospital, as I could manage the situation at home better if I was not there all the time. In June 1958, having qualified as a Midwife, I travelled down by train to Halton in Buckinghamshire to join Princess Mary's RAF Nursing Service, thereafter being a "P.M."

Chapter 6
Air Force Days

I arrived at RAF Halton, which was a few miles from Aylesbury, as a qualified Nurse and Midwife and holding an Orthopaedic Nursing Certificate, in June 1958 with 9 other new entrants. We were all given the rank of Flying Officer and once again were new girls in a strange environment. Our uniforms were waiting for us – stiff white dresses, fastened with tiny pearl buttons, caps which were large and diamond-shaped when made-up, "sleeves" which were removed for patient care, and Air Force blue capes. Our shoes were white and had to kept that way – with great difficulty. We had also been provided with a suit for outdoor use, a Crombie overcoat and a very smart tricorn hat. Our first few days were concerned with familiarisation, and square-bashing. Apparently, new girls always caused onlookers a great deal of amusement at their attempts to march!

After a few days, we were all despatched to various wards and I was sent to the maternity unit. All Air Force hospitals had children's and families' wards for the dependants of the serving men and women. It was a nasty shock suddenly being treated as a qualified and experienced Midwife, although not entirely unexpected. As Pupil Midwives, we had not been allowed to do "episiotomies" – the cutting of the perineum at the time of delivery to facilitate birth. As Midwives, we were expected to be proficient! After 2 days on day duty, during which time I managed to miss all the deliveries, I was put on night duty, in sole charge of the maternity unit, for 21 consecutive nights. This, we decided later, was a "make or break" situation and cannot be comprehended by today's nurses. During that time, with the help of a Nursing Auxiliary, I had total responsibility for everything that happened during a 12-hour shift for 3 weeks. Very soon, I was faced with the "episiotomy" problem.

Wearing 'Blues' (the outdoor uniform) as a Sister in the PMRAFNS, 1958

When it became obvious that help was necessary for a young woman about to have her first baby at 2.00 in the morning, I held my breath, put in the scissors, gave an enormous snip, and out came the baby, crying lustily. I had to summon the doctor on call to suture and it just so happened that the doctor on call that night was a Wing Commander – the Senior Consultant in charge of the unit. We prepared the patient and the necessary equipment, the Wing Commander scrubbed up, sat down and examined the damage. He gave me a very old-fashioned look and I examined my handiwork properly for the first time. I saw that my "enormous snip" was in fact a little cut about 1" long but there was a similar tear on the other side. Muttering something about it looking like a pair of sailor's trousers, and inexperienced midwives, he set to work to repair the damage. It was a case of learning the hard way but the patient healed well and was none the worse and the Consultant was quite nice about it later.

At long last, 21 nights came to an end and it was so good to be back in the land of the living, eating at normal times, going to bed at night instead of trying to sleep during the day, and getting to know my colleagues.

I had arranged to buy a Lambretta from one of the other Pupil Midwives in Camberwell and now I heard that it was being despatched, by rail, from Manchester to Wendover, our nearest station, and just a couple of miles down the road. On the appointed day, I walked down to the station to collect it. It had arrived and was waiting for me in the Station Master's office. I wheeled it on to the platform, having signed for it, and tried to start it. I was beginning to get very frustrated with it when a porter pointed out that the petrol had had to be emptied out for it to travel by train. Of course! So I wheeled my scooter down the road to a garage, with great difficulty, and filled the tank with 2-stroke petrol Although I had seen the machine before and approved it, I had never ridden it and really had no idea how to cope with it. I attached "L" plates, got on, started it, and to my surprise it started straight away. Fortunately, by then it was early evening, and there was not much traffic about as I wobbled up the hill. I signalled correctly, and turned right into the RAF base. Then, as I approached the nursing officers' mess, I realised that I had no idea how to stop. As the wall got nearer and nearer, in desperation I took my hands off everything and fell off, just in time. The machine wasn't damaged but my pride was. After that,

I was able to practice safely and became a little more efficient. And it gave me independence.

In December, I was posted to RAF Wilmslow in Cheshire. Having sent my luggage on by train, I travelled on the Lambretta from Buckinghamshire to Cheshire without mishap but with enormous relief on arriving safely. Wilmslow was the unit where "other ranks" started their training, so the small hospital was there primarily to deal with the new recruits who had reacted badly to their injections. One lad, in bed with a very swollen arm and a high temperature, had only been in the RAF a week but it had been impressed on him that he must always salute Officers. I had to explain to him that this was not necessary while he was a patient and wearing pyjamas.

The atmosphere at Wilmslow was very relaxed and it was a pleasant life. During a stint on night duty (only 2 weeks this time) I was doing a round of the wards in the small hours of the morning. I went over to the infectious diseases block, and was assailed by the smell of burning rubber. I found a young aircraftsman, supposedly on duty, sitting in the kitchen and fast asleep with his plimsolls in the lit gas oven, trying to keep warm!

I had only been at Wilmslow a few weeks when I was posted again at the end of January 1959 to RAF Ely, to "special" a senior officer with polio. I was selected, it transpired later, because of my orthopaedic training but what the powers that be didn't realise was that in an orthopaedic hospital we only ever saw cases of polio once the acute phase had passed. However, my new patient was not badly affected by the disease and made a good recovery. So I was moved to the maternity unit. This was a very busy and happy unit and I got great experience.

As spring approached, I was able to get out and about on days off into the flat Fenlands. As the weather improved and I had a few days off, I decided to ride the Lambretta up to Hull. This was, of course, long before the Humber Bridge was built and to cross the river one had to take the ferry from Barton-on-Humber. To actually reach the ferry, there was a very scary ride along a narrow track with a railway line on one side and the river on the other. It was much worse a year or so later, in the dark, in a car!

In June 1959, I was told that I was to be posted to RAF Wegberg in Germany a few weeks later. Because I could not take the Lambretta with me, I had to sell it. Before I finally parted with it, two of us decided to explore the countryside a little and set off for Sandringham. Jean had a Vespa and we travelled in convoy. We stopped for a pub lunch and then saw threatening and approaching thunder clouds. We soon found ourselves in the middle of a storm, and with thunder crashing around us, we were soon drenched. We were not too far from Hunstanton on the coast and so we headed there, found a café, parked the scooters and ordered tea. We tried to dry our sopping gloves by placing them round the teapot but they merely steamed. We both went into the ladies cloakroom, to sort ourselves out a bit, and in the lavatory bowl I saw the words "Improved Vespa". Jean and I had had a bit of rivalry regarding our respective machines, so this seemed to clinch things! Eventually, she too saw the funny side. So safely back to Ely, without seeing Sandringham.

I only had a week or so left before going abroad and the time passed very quickly, with packing again, and saying farewells. To reach Wegberg, first I had to go to Liverpool Street Station to collect my travel warrant and then travel first class to Harwich. There were 3 other PMs, all of us posted abroad for the first time. We boarded the ferry for the Hook of Holland and then discovered that between us, we were responsible for the general welfare of a large group of airwomen, also posted abroad for the first time. We had a busy night as we crossed the North Sea, as most of the girls expected to be seasick and many were. Once we reached Holland in the morning, everyone felt better, and we could relax a little. We boarded a train for Munchen Gladbach and then went on to Wegberg by RAF bus.

The hospital was attractively designed, with the wards spanning out from a central block, and between each ward there were flower beds bursting with colour in high summer. The officers' mess was a mixed one but the female officers had their own sleeping block, which was a hut containing around 30 single rooms. They were very comfortable but the beds presented a real problem in that, in German fashion, they were built in, making it extremely difficult to change sheets, let alone turn mattresses.

The maternity unit here was as far away as it could be – right at the far end of one of the spurs. It consisted of an ante-natal ward, a labour ward, a post-natal ward, a nursery and a special care baby unit. It was always busy and usually hectic. Things were not too bad during the day, when the staffing levels were quite high, but on night duty, there was just one Midwife and one German Nursing Auxiliary.

Looking back, I don't know how we managed – caring for mothers in for rest, for those in labour, for those who had just been delivered, a nursery full of noisy babies and babies needing special care. Some of these babies were tiny premature infants and others were undergoing exchange transfusions because their mothers were Rhesus Negative. At least time passed very quickly, but sometimes one could still be there at 10.00 in the morning, utterly exhausted and desperate for bed, writing up the notes and reports if it had been a particularly busy night. If one had had the misfortune to have to call a doctor out to suture, for a forceps delivery, or a Caesarean Section it was even worse, but it made us very good at assessing situations and decision making. It was very good experience.

Fortunately, we did have quite generous periods of leave and with the rest of Europe on our doorstep, we had wonderful opportunities for travel. In common with most of my colleagues, I bought my first car out there – a bright red Renault Dauphine – and started having driving lessons from a corporal in the transport section. Because so many of us were learning to drive, our Matron panicked a little and warned us that we might have to take the German Civil Driving Test which included, apart from driving, a German written test and an oral about the workings of the engine. This proved to be an unfounded rumour and in due course, most of us took and passed the RAF driving test. We were then free to tear all over Europe, belting up the autobahns, but we were not permitted to drive in the UK until we had taken the British test.

Most of us took advantage of the chances to travel. During my first winter, a party of us went by train to Zermatt for skiing. It was great fun until we returned and I realised that I had picked up a bug. I had to be admitted, back in Wegberg, for the problem to be identified as intestinal parasites. It became a recurring nuisance until it was finally resolved over 20 years later. On other occasions, I drove North with a good friend Mary Coram to Denmark, and with Olive Kirkham I drove right down to the South of France. We were able to travel freely, without booking anywhere and with a cold bag in the back for butter, cheese, tomatoes, and a daily visit to a local baker, we were free agents. All we needed otherwise was a good map, a phrase book and a spirit of adventure.

Wegberg was quite close to the Dutch border and we could cross over very easily for flowers on a Sunday morning or for a weekend in Amsterdam or Rotterdam. Despite the desperately heavy workload, being in Germany was great fun and we were young enough to enjoy it and make the most of it. It was also a little unsettling, as people were constantly being posted out and posted in. In July 1961, I learnt that I was due to be posted back to England, to Nocton Hall, near Lincoln. Having sent my luggage on, I drove to Rotterdam and took the ferry to Hull. I had a few days' leave before going to Nocton Hall and I had arranged to take my UK driving test during this time. I had to have a few lessons to rid me of the bad habits I had picked up tearing over Europe, but having passed, I was then able to arrive independently.

Having by now spent 3 years in the RAF, there were some familiar faces to greet me, which meant that one could settle into a new routine more quickly. Again, I was despatched to the maternity unit but here it was nothing like as hectic as Wegberg had been. Our mess was in the original hall, which was a building of great beauty and character, and the grounds were well-laid out and colourful. The hospital had been built in the grounds and consisted of hutted wards. We never lacked the latest equipment, and being well-staffed, it meant that we could give our patients the best possible care. One of my Midwife colleagues was Mary Johnston and we became good friends, with a shared sense of humour and the ridiculous. We went on several holidays together. One summer, we drove to Dover, put the car on the ferry, and then on the train in France, and travelled in style as far as Lyons. There we drove the car off the train and over the Pyrenees into Spain and the Costa Brava. We had not booked anywhere but as few travellers went to that part of Spain in the early 60s, we had no problems. A highlight was staying in the beautiful hamlet of Agua Blava – a small collection of houses and a hotel right off the beaten track and on a very wild bit of coastline. We explored the coast and diverted to see the monastery at Monserrat, and then on to Barcelona before heading north towards Toulouse. On the way, we discovered that our maps were out of date and a road marked on the map turned out to be a dried-up river bed, which we had to follow for several hours before it turned back into a road. Travelling then was still unpredictable and an adventure.

On another occasion, Mary and I drove up to Scotland. The MacRobert family owned a large estate near the banks of the River Dee but during the war, all the sons of the family lost their lives while serving in the RAF. Consequently, after the war, Lady MacRobert decided to make her home available as a rest centre, available to those with whom her sons would have lived and worked, had they survived.

It was called Alastrean House and quickly became very popular as a place to go for a break, being very luxurious, well-appointed and very reasonable. It was also set in beautiful surroundings and not far from the Dee, Balmoral, and Crathie church. While we were staying there, Mary and I discussed an advertisement we had seen in the *Nursing Times* for a team of nurses to work in Ankara in Turkey. This would mean resigning our commissions but it seemed to be a great challenge, to improve the standards of nursing in a developing country, as well as an adventure. If we decided to apply, we would be interviewed by the Department of Technical Co-operation (later to become the Ministry of Overseas Development) but co-opted to the Turkish Department of Health. We weighed up the situation, both in Scotland and on our return to Nocton Hall, and then went ahead and put in our applications.

In the meantime, Patrick had graduated from Durham University with a B.Sc. in Agriculture; had spent 2 years in Southern Rhodesia as it was then, and while he was there, decided to be ordained. He had returned to England, gone to Mirfield College for theological training, and been ordained Deacon. His first assignment was as Curate to the Vicar in Kirby Moorside, Yorkshire, with his new wife Pauline. Their daughter Bridget was born in 1959 while I was in Germany. After a couple of years, they decided to accept the challenge of living and working abroad, and went to Borneo. Here, Patrick established a farm school, for 6 days out of 7, but on Sundays he took services for the Christian Community. It was a difficult life for the whole family and Pauline, particularly, did not adjust easily to it. Patrick was affected by the climate but nonetheless, Stephen was born in Singapore in 1961. My parents became accustomed to their offspring travelling to obscure places but they made no attempts to dissuade either of us. Mary's parents, on the other hand, were not at all happy at the thought of their only daughter going to Turkey. Her father was not at all well and her mother was an anxious lady at the best of times. However, we were both summoned to London for an interview and subsequently offered places in a team of 5 British nurses going to Ankara as Clinical Instructors in Nursing.

We accepted and then had a great flurry of activity as we resigned our commissions and started to plan what we needed to take with us. We were told that we would be given help in finding accommodation but that meant that we had to consider all the basics necessary for independent living – sheets, towels, crockery and cutlery, as well as clothing. Then we had to decide what could be sent in advance and what we would have to take with us. It was an exciting and alarming time, going into the unknown, and it was made worse by the fact that we had been promised a course in basic Turkish before we left and it never materialised. We knew that we were expected to teach Turkish Student Nurses the basics of patient care, but without the language, it was going to be difficult.

We flew from Heathrow in July 1963, very smart in suits, hats and gloves, as befitted young professional ladies at that time. We refuelled in Athens and then came in to land in Istanbul. The journey had taken all day and as we circled the city, we saw, very dramatically, the outline and lights of the city on one hand, and on the other, a very clear night sky full of stars and a very new moon. Here, we changed planes and flew on to Ankara.

Outside the Mess RAF Hospital Wegberg, Germany, 1961

Chapter 7
Turkish Days

We spent the first few days in a hotel in Ankara, getting our bearings and trying to find a suitable flat. It was July and extremely hot. Foolishly, I had brought out clothes which packed easily but were made of man-made fibres, rendering them totally unsuited to the heat and humidity. Mary was tall and as we tramped the streets of Ankara looking at possible flats, I tried to walk in her shadow to escape the worst of the midday sun. I have never liked excessive heat.

With help from the staff at the British Embassy, we were given the name of a likely Turkish landlord and within a few days, we had agreed to move in to one of his flats in the district of Kavaklidere. This was a pleasant residential area, being developed, and fairly near the Embassy. The rent of the flat was being paid by the British Government, so we were not in a position to argue too much. But it was in fact a pleasant flat, on the 4th floor (no lift) and it had a large and sunny sitting room, 2 bedrooms, a kitchen, a bathroom with a loo, with a separate loo next door, and a storage room. In theory, it was splendid. In practice, things were rather different. The second loo was the "hole in the ground" type, which we reserved for Turkish visitors and cleaning materials. The kitchen was overrun with cockroaches and thanks to the local plumbing, it was a lottery whether water or sewage came out of the taps. Fortunately, one could buy large bottles of drinking water from the street vendors. The call of "su" for water caused a rush of flat-dwellers to rush down and queue at the cart.

We had a few days to get ourselves organised before we had to think about work, so we were able to explore the neighbourhood shops. In 1963, supermarkets were just getting established in Turkey, which was a great boon for us as our Turkish was still virtually non-existent.

Instead, we could wander down the aisles looking at the labels on the tins and the pictures on the packets to sort out the contents. The local greengrocer was a different matter altogether, as we not only had to learn the Turkish for the fruit and vegetables, we also had to start thinking in metric weights. Consequently, during that first week, I asked for 2 kilos of "fasulye" (very nice-looking runner beans) thinking I was asking for half a pound. He gave me a funny look as he reached for the largest paper bag in the shop and slowly filled it to the top. I realised my mistake but I didn't know how to say "stop". The beans kept us going for quite a while...

The time came to start work. Our contracts from the Department of Technical Co-operation were with the Turkish Ministry of Health and we had been employed as Clinical Instructors to teach basic nursing to Turkish student nurses. This was fine in theory but on our very first visit to the Ankara Hospital we learnt that the students came under the Turkish Ministry of Education. We met the very fierce Director of the School of Nursing and understood that she was certainly not going to permit her students to come into contact with interfering foreign women if she could help it. Impasse. We were welcomed on to the wards but that defeated the object, as the students only came on to the wards twice a week, and then in large numbers. The situation was further complicated by the fact that the students were only 14 years old, very immature, knew no English, and as yet we had virtually no Turkish. Within a week or so of our arrival, we were joined by 2 further members of our team – Jane King-Wilkinson (also from St. Thomas's) and Marjorie Scott. Assuming that we might sometime be allowed to teach, we had to decide on our specialities. Mary opted for the surgical wards, Marjorie for the medical, Jane for the paediatric and I had the maternity wards. Marjorie and Jane had found flats close to ours and having arranged our hours of duty with the Head Nurse (or Matron), she provided us with a small sitting room and helped us to find a taxi driver who would take us to and from the hospital. He was called Osman Bey and he became a good friend. Having organised our uniforms, we were ready to face the wards and the patients, feeling very much like junior nurses. The language barrier was our greatest problem, as we could not communicate with the staff or patients, and we were not able to clarify our position as Clinical Instructors. Turkish lessons were arranged for us and we learnt the basics quite quickly, even if we could not construct sentences.

But our biggest shock was the state of the wards. To say that they were filthy was an understatement. Bedding was rarely changed between patients, and when it was, it was tossed into a laundry chute along with soiled dressings. The chute was blocked most days because nobody removed the contents in the basement. With obstetric patients, the problem was quite dreadful, sheets inevitably being soiled and stained, and to see a new patient admitted to a bed just vacated by someone else was an intolerable and frustrating situation as there was so little that we could do. I quickly learnt the Turkish for "very dirty" but the Turks just smiled indulgently. One or two of the doctors had travelled and worked abroad but they seemed to see nothing wrong with the standards of hygiene or of nursing care. Our first few weeks we all found very depressing and disheartening, as we seemed unable to make any sort of impact.

As our command of Turkish improved slowly with our weekly lessons, things improved a little in that we could communicate, and our inevitable mistakes caused a great deal of amusement. We established a routine: Osman Bey would collect us about 7.00 and drive us to the hospital for 7.30. We travelled in mufti and changed on arrival, and then went to our various areas of work. We decided that we would not work at weekends, at least until our roles were better established. We had a coffee break in our sitting room during the morning and later had lunch there, which we brought from home. Once or twice we tried lunch in the hospital staff dining room but found it quite unacceptable, as the standards in the kitchens were no better than elsewhere. Osman Bey, who was one of the nicest people we met in Turkey, collected us at 4.30, and with enormous relief, we returned every day to our flats and a little normality.

The Head Nurse, or Matron, was quite a pleasant lady, and seemed to understand our difficulties in adjusting to a different way of life. However, she made it quite clear, mostly by mime, that she did not approve of English women with bare legs, despite the heat, and expected us to wear stockings. This came as a bit of a shock when we thought of the standards on the wards but we complied. There did not appear to be Ward Sisters, as we knew them, and certainly there was no routine on the wards. However, each ward had a cleaner of sorts and these amazing ladies kept catheters in their pockets, along with other bits of medical equipment, and gave enemas and catheterised patients as required...

A meeting was at last arranged for us with the Director of Nursing, in the School of Nursing, to see if we could be permitted to fulfil our proper roles of teaching students. Very reluctantly, she agreed that twice a week we could each have an allocation of about 15 students. This was quite contrary to the practice in England, where perhaps 2 students would be allocated to a ward for 2 or 3 months, during which time they would be part of the ward team. One could get to know them and build up a relationship. With the Turkish system, they were not part of the team, they only worked straight shifts (finishing at 4.30 every day) so they never experienced what might happen during the evening or night, and they never had to take responsibility. Attempting to teach 15 giggly young girls in a foreign language was well nigh impossible but we did the best we could and laughed at ourselves whenever possible. One of my extra problems was the nursery. The babies were mostly kept in the nursery during the day and taken out to their mothers for the night. The practice seemed to be to change them once a day, otherwise they were swaddled, and during the day, instead of being fed by their mothers, the nursery nurse, Hava, filled a feeding bottle with sugar and water from the tap, and went from baby to baby with the same teat, refilling the bottle as it became empty. I tried very hard to change the system, and if Hava saw me coming, she would quickly change the teat and announce, in fractured English: "Me very very GOOD nurse." And this became the crux of the problem. The Turkish nurses would attempt to adhere to better practices simply to please us and not because they could see the principles behind them.

We persevered and did our best and decided that to compensate, we should have as much fun as possible during our time off. We got to know quite a few people in the embassy and as a result were invited to parties and receptions. One of our main delights, during our lunchtime, was planning holidays and breaks to make the most of being in Turkey.

As the weather became cooler, and with our routines established, I started thinking about getting a car. I had had to sell my Renault Dauphine on leaving England and I longed to be independent again. I heard that one of the secretaries at the embassy was about to be posted to Denmark and wanted to sell her car before leaving. The car was a Singer Gazelle, 2 years old, and in very good condition, not having been used much. I agreed to buy it but soon discovered that things were not quite that simple. There was a great deal of Turkish red tape to cut through, especially as the owner had diplomatic immunity and therefore the registration number could not be passed on to me. It was quite difficult getting expert advice from England, as the post took several days, and getting through by phone was almost impossible. My father had a friend in the insurance business and he agreed, reluctantly, to provide me with insurance cover, but only when I had sorted out the registration number. While these problems were being resolved, the car was impounded. I could not trace the original number and I seemed to have reached stalemate until a helpful Turk, who worked in the embassy as a driver, told me that he had found a pair of rusty old number plates in the embassy garage. With a little baksheesh, I got the number plates, the insurance cover was issued from England, the red tape was finally severed and the car was released from the pound – with a very flat battery. More Turkish lira ensured a tow to the Embassy, where the battery was charged, and finally, after over 4 months, I drove it down the hill to Kavaklidere. There was great excitement among the team, as at last we could go off on short trips.

Our first trip was almost our last. The four of us arranged to visit a hotel by a lake for the weekend. It was highly recommended and was just 60 miles out of Ankara. A few miles out of the city, the tarmac road ceased abruptly, being replaced by dusty tracks full of potholes. The standard of driving was quite terrifying and more than once, I was pushed off the road by drivers overtaking at speed. After about 20 miles, I was aware of a strange smell like fried onions and then saw smoke billowing out behind. It seemed expedient to stop. It appeared that a stone had shot up and burst the oil sump. We all got out of the car, feeling very vulnerable. Eventually, Jane and Marjorie flagged down a bus and said they would wait for us at the nearest village. Mary and I stayed with the car. There was not much passing traffic but after half an hour, a large Ford drew up and offered to tow us to the nearest village. His car was full of people, including granny in the back. With a very short rope fixed to our bumper, we set off, at a terrifying speed, over dirt roads, and far too close to each other for comfort. Mary said that granny kept smiling at us through the back window but I dare not take my hands off the wheel or my foot hovering over the brake. The journey took perhaps 20 minutes and we were left in a state of shock at the village garage where Jane and Marjorie were waiting. The mechanic implied that he could repair it, despite it being Saturday afternoon, and he set to. We bought some warm beer and cold ice cream and waited. The repair took over an hour and having settled up, we decided to continue our journey to the hotel. We had a very pleasant break and returned safely, and cautiously, to Ankara the following day. That repair proved to be so good that it was still there when I sold the car over 2 years later, having driven it back to England.

Towards the end of 1963 we had been joined by the fifth member of our team. The embassy staff told us that someone called Clara was coming and we had visions of an elderly lady, possibly set in her ways, and it was with some apprehension that we all went to the airport to meet her. In fact, her name was Clare and she was young, pretty, and ready to take on the young Turks!

During our 2-year contract to work in Turkey, we certainly made the most of our opportunities to travel and our journeys compensated a little for the frustrations at work. In early 1964, Mary and I flew to Athens and joined a cruise round the Greek Islands. It was my first experience of cruising, though certainly not the last. The ship was Greek, and very comfortable, and to see the islands in the spring, covered with wild flowers, was an unforgettable experience. We visited Mykonos, Delos, Santorini, Rhodes and Patmos, as well as seeing a bit of Athens before we sailed (and spending a night by mistake in high class brothel!).

In the summer of 1964, Jane, Marjorie, Mary and I joined a party of Americans based in Ankara who were planning to sail up the Bosphorus and along the Black Sea. We went overnight to Istanbul by train. The station terminus was on the Asian shore and we had the unforgettable sight, as we crossed over by ferry, of the Istanbul skyline silhouetted against the early morning sky. After lunch, we boarded the Turkish cargo ship which also took about 30 passengers. The first night on board, our tour leader, a lady of uncertain years in Bermuda shorts, gathered us all together after dinner for coffee in the saloon. She asked us all to say who we were, where we came from, and what we had done that we were proud of. We English greeted this with a marked lack of enthusiasm and Jane ended by saying that she had done nothing she was proud of. We quickly realised that there was a great gulf of misunderstanding between us and our American cousins. All the other passengers were American, apart from a German couple.

Sailing up the Bosphorus was fascinating. We passed old wooden buildings and ancient castles, and it all looked very beautiful and romantic. When we reached the far end, we turned right, as it were, and headed into the Black Sea. We spent several very interesting days

The team in Turkey.
(Left to right) Mary, the author, Jane, Marjorie and Clare, 1964.

Ankara, 1965.
Back: Turkish Head Nurse and Deputy.
Front: Clare, Mary and the author.

calling in at little ports and taking on cargo or dropping it off. At Giresun, it was the start of the cherry season and to celebrate the first cargo of cherries being put aboard, sheep were slaughtered on the quayside. I was the only passenger who refused to watch. We continued east, calling in at Trabzon (Trebizond in Rose Macaulay's book), and after several days of sailing, we approached the town of Hopa, very close to the Russian border, where the crew was scheduled to change. Because of this, we were told that dinner would not be available on board. So with the ship anchored in the harbour, all the passengers were taken ashore by tender to find a meal. There was very little to see in the town and only one restaurant, which did very good business. While we were still eating, the weather deteriorated, it became very windy, and soon the rain was coming down in torrents. At first, nobody seemed very concerned but the storm increased in intensity, it was getting late, and the restaurant wished to close. Someone suggested that we could seek refuge in a bank along the road which, surprisingly, was open, although it was by now approaching midnight. The bank provided very basic amenities – a "hole-in-the-ground" toilet and a cold water tap. There was an area where most of us could sit, presumably where customers normally waited for their money. There were no bank officials around and certainly no money!

We could see our ship, about half a mile offshore, but the crew having changed over before the storm broke, there was now no way they could come to collect us. Periodically, some of us would go to the door to assess the ferocity of the wind and suddenly, the German lady shrieked: "Zee ship, she sail!" Sure enough, the ship, all lit up, was moving slowly westwards. The German lady and many of the Americans became quite hysterical as we realised that we were now in the bank in Hopa for the night. There were 30 of us, with no food, one toilet, dodgy water and not a toothbrush or a bar of soap between us. We tried to stay calm and for some reason, now forgotten, we had a pack of cards, so we played whist. Unfortunately, after half an hour or so, the lights began to flicker and fade, and when we could no longer tell a black card from a red one, we had to pack it in. We dozed fitfully, either sitting up on straight chairs, or lying on the hard floor.

In the morning, tour leader came into her own. The storm had abated a little, although the seas were running high. She went into the town at daybreak and managed, although her Turkish was very limited, to buy some bread and to hire a coach. The plan was that we could travel along

Ankara, 1965.
Head Nurse, Medical Director, the Author, Mary and Marjorie

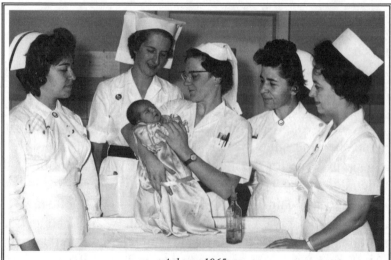

Ankara, 1965.
Deputy Head Nurse, Mary, the Author, Head Nurse, Marjorie

the coast to the next port and then re-board. However, the "coach" was extremely ancient, very decrepit and full of rust and broken-down seats. But the engine worked and there was a driver. We were a subdued and sorry-looking lot as we piled in. We drove a few miles along the coast to Rize but we could see our ship, again anchored offshore. The seas were still too high for us to be taken out. Then tour leader had a really bright idea – as we had time in hand, we could go round the local tea factory. Having been horribly shaken up on the trip from Hopa to Rize, we now had the thrill of watching machinery sorting out tea leaves with a similar sort of shake, except this was side to side, instead of up and down. Nobody really fancied lunch as we climbed dismally back into the bus and headed off towards Trabzon. The ship was there but still offshore and the sea was still rough. Eventually, we carried on to Samsun, where the ship was able to dock in the harbour. It was with enormous relief that we went back on board, grubby and hungry, over 24 hours after leaving it.

Because the trip had been delayed by the storm, we were given the option of returning late to Istanbul or travelling straight back to Ankara by bus. By a majority decision, we opted to return by bus as some of us had to return to work. So the following evening, we set off on a hair-raising journey through the night, from the Black Sea to Ankara. This vehicle was certainly younger than the previous one but still pretty ancient. What really alarmed us, though, was the casual way the driver filled up with petrol with a cigarette hanging out of his mouth. We expected to be blown up at any minute. But we made it safely back to Ankara and one of the enduring memories is of us all standing bleary-eyed on the pavement in the cold light of early dawn while tour leader asked us to applaud our driver.

Our next trip, some months later, was not nearly so exciting until it was almost over. Olive, still a good friend from our PM days, had been posted to Cyprus and for some time we had been trying to arrange a trip together. The difficulties were made worse by the political situation in Cyprus at that time and by her Matron who put all sorts of objections in her way but eventually, Olive received special permission to fly to Turkey, with a very firm deadline for her return. We booked a cruise, again on a Turkish cargo boat, travelling from Istanbul and along the Mediterranean coast as far as Alexandria and back. Olive duly flew in to Ankara, where Mary and I met her and took her back to our flat for the night. The following day we went to Istanbul by train and embarked.

Again, the ship was small, with only 30 passengers on board, and the cabins were spartan but adequate. We travelled down through the Sea of Marmara into the Mediterranean and turned east. We called in to Bodrum – still a very unspoilt little fishing village with a superb crusader castle – and on to Fethiye, Antalya, Mersin, and Iskenderun. We had wonderful views of towns, ruins and the Taurus Mountains. Our last port of call on the return journey was Izmir – another really interesting city, with a great deal of history. As we sailed back towards Istanbul, with only a relatively short distance to cover, we stopped at dusk to pick up a large contingent of Turkish soldiers. We really thought nothing of this, as the soldiers were not permitted to mix with the passengers. We were due to dock in Istanbul early the following morning; we had a flight booked from Istanbul back to Ankara which would give Olive plenty of time to return to the flat with us, and pick up some of her belongings before flying back to Cyprus before her deadline expired. We had it all worked out, in theory.

During that last night on board, the soldiers were involved in extensive manoeuvres. The ship kept stopping, as small groups of men were put ashore and left, presumably to find their own way back. In consequence, at daybreak, instead of coming in to dock in Istanbul, we were still out at sea, passing slowly through the Dardanelles. This was our "worst-case" scenario. Olive knew, and we knew, that if she did not return to Cyprus that day, her future was very seriously in jeopardy. We were helpless, as the crew could not, or would not, understand our dilemma. We should have docked at 8.00, and the flight was scheduled for noon. As we slowly approached the docking area, time was passing too quickly. At 11.00, we were standing, with all our luggage, watching as the strip of water between us and the dock slowly, so slowly, diminished. Once we were in shouting distance, we hollered for a taxi and by 11.30, although we still had not docked, we could see the taxi waiting. We were helped ashore at the first possible moment, piled our luggage and ourselves into the taxi, and said what one should never say to a Turkish taxi driver: "chabuk" – which means "quickly". We had 20 minutes to reach the airport and catch the plane and we had 10 miles to go…

He did go quickly. We reached the airport on the stroke of noon and saw our plane taking off as we roared into the airport…

This was classed as one of the worst moments in our lives. We were stranded in an airport, with a deadline approaching, and the inevitable language problems. When it seemed that we had really reached rock bottom and could see no solution to our nightmare, a guardian angel appeared. He was a wealthy Turkish businessman, about to return to Ankara that afternoon in his own private plane. Our problems had obviously flashed around the airport and he offered to take us with him. So we travelled, in a very small plane, at very low altitudes, and at a very modest speed, back to Ankara. By the skin of her teeth, and with half an hour to spare, Olive made it back to Cyprus before the clock struck midnight and her deadline expired.

Our next big adventure was returning to England. Our 2 years were up in July 1965 and Mary and I decided that we would return by road, in the Singer Gazelle. I wrote, with tongue in cheek, to the AA in England for a route. When it arrived, it took us through Bulgaria, which we had been warned locally to avoid. So I planned my own route, which would take us across Turkey, into Greece and on through Yugoslavia, Austria, Germany and Holland, to catch the ferry from Rotterdam to Hull. We arranged to send our heavy luggage by sea. The question of insurance for the car arose again and after a great deal of research, at last we discovered what the original registration number of the car had been, before it acquired CD plates. This meant that while I was driving round Turkey with the number plates from the Embassy garage, with insurance to match, I had to have insurance to match the correct number plates by the time I arrived in England. This put the very upright friend of my father in a very difficult position, as he was now being asked to produce a second set of documents for the same car. My father was also a man of probity and how he persuaded his friend to undertake something somewhat dishonest, I shall never know. The essential paperwork duly arrived, with veiled warnings of the possible consequences.

And so the time came for us to leave Turkey. During our 2 years, we all felt that we had done very little to improve the standards of nursing care but the opposition to our endeavours had been enormous. We had done our best and had compensated our frustrations by making the most of our free time while we were in such an interesting part of the world. So, on different occasions we had visited Goreme, with its lunar landscape and cave dwellings; seen the Whirling Dervishes in action in Konya before they were withdrawn from public view; bathed in the chalky pools at night in Pammukale above Denizli; flown to Cyprus before it was a divided island; and flown to Beirut when it was still a beautiful and elegant city. From here, we went by taxi to Damascus and on to Jerusalem. We knew at the time that we were fortunate to have the opportunity to see so much and we made the most of it. And it was educational!

And so, very early one July morning, we left Ankara and were escorted to the main road to Istanbul by a very tearful Osman Bey, our Turkish taxi driver. He had been a very good friend and had helped us in all sorts of ways, including improving our knowledge of the language. He was a patient and gentle man – unusual in a Turk. The Singer was loaded down with our luggage and last-minute presents. The "alternative" number plates and insurance documents were very well hidden. We spent a night in Istanbul and then had an uneventful journey through the European part of Turkey and into Greece, with very superficial formalities at the border. We had not booked any accommodation for our journey, as so much depended on the state of the roads. We spent the next night in a small hotel in Thessaloniki and on the following day, crossed the border into Yugoslavia. Initially, the roads were quite good and very quiet. We stopped for lunch by a lake and parked in a dense wood by the road. I reversed the car into the wood and while Mary was preparing lunch at the front, I was working at the back, with a screwdriver and a number plate. Then I turned the car round and worked on the front, well out of sight of any passing traffic. When the job was done, and when nobody was around, we tossed the old number plates deep into the lake. Finally, we had a ceremonial burning of the now irrelevant insurance documents. Then, having had lunch and feeling like something out of a James Bond movie, we continued north. At least, and at last, we were "legal"!

We did not really relax until we crossed the border into Austria, where at last we felt as though we were back in civilisation. Our onward journey across Germany and into Holland was uneventful, the Singer behaved well and the roads, increasingly, were good. We spent 5 days over the journey, travelling an average of 300 miles a day. As we approached Rotterdam, we felt an enormous sense of achievement, and indeed, it was an adventure for 2 single women to drive from Asia and across Europe in 1965. But we had one final hiccup. As we drove into Rotterdam, the most appalling noise erupted from the back of the car. I stopped, got out, had a look and burst out laughing. The cobbled streets of the city had loosened my handiwork and the noise was the sound of the rear number plate being dragged over the cobbles. Having screwed it up, we carried on to the docks, parked the car and rang England. We had not wanted to tempt providence by phoning during the journey but all we had to do now was get ourselves and the car on the overnight ferry and be transported across the North Sea to Hull overnight.

The following morning was very emotional, as we disembarked, greeted my parents and Mary's brother, and watched anxiously as the Singer was removed by crane.

Mary had decided sometime previously that she would return to the P.M.s when we came back but I wanted to venture further up the ladder. But first, after a few days at home, I had arranged to go to Patrick.

Following their return to England, their marriage in Sarawak having been put under a great strain, all was not well. He was appointed to Kirbymoorside, still in North Yorkshire, as Vicar, and they tried to patch things up. After a year or so, Patrick was offered the living at Ampleforth with Oswaldkirk, which he accepted but Pauline declined to join him. She stayed in a cottage in Kirbymoorside with the children. It was into this traumatic situation that I returned from Turkey and I offered to stay with him for a while until things sorted themselves out a bit. The vicarage at Ampleforth, although not old, was not a comfortable building, having draughty windows, basic equipment and a general air of neglect but the most wonderful views. Here, we both tried to review our respective futures.

Chapter 8
Ampleforth Days

Living with Patrick was quite a novelty after Turkey. Like most men, he was very untidy but he was also distraught, his wife and children having left him, and he was also trying to re-acclimatise himself to England and rural parish duties after working overseas.

I found myself a job quite quickly, as a "Generalised Duties District Nurse", which meant caring for people in their own homes in a wide area of the North Riding. I was the District Nurse, District Midwife and School Nurse, visiting 4 local schools in the glorious countryside around Ampleforth. I sold the faithful Singer Gazelle and bought myself a Mini and soon people came to know us as "The Body and Soul Team". We acquired a black Labrador puppy and a dear lady from the village who came in almost every day as a sort of non-resident housekeeper. She was a very gentle, motherly, sweet-natured lady known to all as "Nan", and her cooking was superb. Her presence caused my mother great anguish on her fairly frequent visits, when she realised that we were coping between us and without her.

Unfortunately, Pauline was not prepared to return to Patrick, causing him great sorrow and heartache. They were not, in fact, a well-matched pair, as they were both very immature when they married and Patrick was too much of an innocent to cope with moods and arguments. The loss of his children grieved him enormously, as Pauline was reluctant to let him have any dealings with them. Legal access was arranged but when they were delivered, reluctantly, at the end of the drive on alternate Saturdays, there were always tears and tantrums. At that time Bridget was 5 and Stephen 3. The visits always seemed to be traumatic for everyone.

In the meantime, Patrick got down to parish duties and quickly became a popular figure around the village. He also had responsibilities for the adjacent village of Oswaldkirk and became immersed in visiting, producing a parish magazine, writing sermons, and after a while, transcribing the old and fragile parish registers.

I realised quite quickly that although I enjoyed caring for patients in their own homes and loved visiting the children in their old-fashioned village schools, I did not want to spend the rest of my working life in the same job. I applied to the Royal College of Nursing in London with a view to taking the year-long course in nursing administration. Most people taking this course were seconded by their hospitals which put me in rather a difficult position, as I could not afford to study for a year without an income. I was fortunate enough to be sponsored by St. Thomas' Hospital, with the promise of a scholarship.

After spending more than a year with Patrick, he seemed more able to cope, with the help of Nan and Bruce the Labrador, so in September 1966 I headed for London.

At that time, it was fairly easy to find accommodation for single women undergoing periods of study and I was recommended to a lovely house in Thurloe Place where several of us were booked for the same course. We each had pleasant rooms and meals were provided for a modest charge. I enjoyed the academic year in London and the stimulation of attending classes, writing up lecture notes, and making some good friends among the 60 or so students. We had intensive lectures on hospital and nursing administration, psychology and public speaking, and we had placements in a variety of hospitals for a week at a time. We usually made these visits in groups of 2 or 3, going from London teaching hospitals to cottage hospitals to enormous psychiatric hospitals. These visits helped us to determine our future directions and also gave us an insight into good and bad practice. One of these visits was to the Friarage Hospital in Northallerton, just before Christmas 1966, and I not only enjoyed this visit but it also gave me the chance to spend Christmas with Patrick in Ampleforth, just a few miles away.

The Spring of 1967 was largely taken up with studying for the exams and applying for jobs. This was the time when the Salmon Report into the future of nursing administration was hitting the headlines, and it was therefore an interesting time to be approaching the bottom rung of the administration ladder. Pilot schemes for Salmon had been set up in a few selected hospitals, with a view to evaluation the following year, followed by possible national implementation. I applied for the new post, under Salmon, of a Number 7, or Nursing Officer, in charge of the maternity unit of St. George's Hospital, at that time at Hyde Park Corner. I was interviewed by that alarming lady, Dame Muriel Powell, who was a leading light in the nursing world, having headed several committees. St. George's had been selected, under her supervision, as one of the hospitals implementing a pilot scheme for Salmon. The post I was applying for would have been described as Assistant Matron under the old scheme. To my surprise, I was offered the post, to start as soon as our exams had finished. I got digs with a friend from the course, who had a flat off the Fulham Palace Road, and with the exams safely behind and passed reasonably well, I started work as a Number 7 at St George's in August 1967.

Chapter 9
Into Administration

It was exciting to be back in London, in a demanding new post, with challenges ahead. It was also interesting to be in at the start of "Salmon" and involved with the implementation of a new system. My predecessor's title was Superintendent Midwife but mine was Nursing Officer Grade 7 (Obstetrics). And although I had total responsibility for the maternity unit, I also had occasional responsibility for the whole hospital, especially during evening shifts, and at weekends.

The unit was busy, with some well-known private patients as well as NHS ladies. The consultants were pleasant and the staff supportive. We had a large number of Jewish patients and consequently ritual circumcisions were performed frequently, which gave an added dimension to a routine day – if a day can ever be routine in a maternity unit. I slipped back into hospital life very easily.

I had only been at St. George's a few months when I spotted an advertisement in the *Nursing Times* which made me catch my breath. It was for a Deputy Matron at the Friarage Hospital in Northallerton, where I had gone during my academic year at the Royal College of Nursing. To me, this was a dream job – a happy hospital, close to Patrick and where Salmon was yet to be implemented. But I had only been at St. George's for 6 months. I decided that it would not hurt to get an information pack and that would give me breathing space to consider my options. In my socks, I knew that I was planning to apply but first I had to face Dame Muriel Powell, previously Matron but now Principal Nursing Officer, or Grade 9, in charge of St. George's. She was not pleased.

I went up to Northallerton for the interview, having been short-listed, and met my parents in the White Hart for lunch as they were interested and hopeful that I might return to Yorkshire. For the interview, I faced the entire hospital management committee, plus Norman Davis, the Hospital Secretary, and Doreen Bayston, the Matron. Because I had nothing to lose, I enjoyed the interview, and it went well. I was offered the post the same day and Mr Davis drove me round to the White Hart to meet my parents and have tea with us. It was all very friendly and augured well. But I still had to return to St.George's, face the music and work my notice.

I moved up to Yorkshire in August 1967, where I was made very welcome and given temporary accommodation in the Rutson Hospital, a little cottage hospital attached to the Friarage, until the Deputy Matron's flat became available. Because the pilot schemes for "Salmon" were not due to be assessed until the following year, the administration was still of the "old school". Apart from the Matron and myself, there were 2 Assistant Matrons and an Administrative Sister, and collectively, we were known as "the book and key brigade". I had to move gently, as 2 members of the team had applied for the job I now had but there did not appear to be too many hard feelings.

The flat became available (it was the upper flat of a purpose-built unit and Miss Bayston had the ground floor flat). We shared a domestic and she shared the gossip! I acquired a car and settled down to country life. At work, I was responsible for the allocation of Student Nurses, ensuring that each one had appropriate training in all wards and departments. This was just up my street and I spent hours in the office and the flat, devising charts and plans.

When I was off duty, I was able to see Patrick most weeks, as Ampleforth was only about 20 miles away, and it was reassuring to see him more settled. After I had been at the Friarage about a year, Miss Bayston announced that she was leaving to marry. This, in fact, was no surprise to me, as I knew that she had been "courting" a local policeman for some time. The flats in which we both lived were not sound-proofed! This was a great event for the hospital and it was interesting to be on the fringes of the appointment of a new Matron. As the candidates came round, we met them and made our own assessments, as no doubt they did of us. Everyone was pleased to hear of the appointment of Margaret Fawley – she was our choice as well as that of the HMC. As she said, she brought her grey hair with her, as she had turned grey at a very early age. So she was younger than she appeared to be – an intelligent lady, with a good sense of humour and a neat turn of phrase. With this change behind us, we all settled down and I was able to hone my administrative skills with the help and support of Margaret Fawley. I could not have wished for a better boss.

But after another year had passed, I was encouraged to consider my future and apply for a more senior post. My first application, to a hospital in Harrogate, was a disaster. I attended the interview in a white suit and managed to spill coffee down it before the formal interviews. I lost my nerve and my chances. My next foray into promotion was to Leicester, where the general hospital was seeking a Matron. Again, I was short-listed and attended a difficult interview. I really did not know, on the journey home, whether I would accept the post if it was offered.

I suppose I was flattered to be offered the post of Matron of Leicester General Hospital. Such an appointment represented the pinnacle of my ambition but I had reservations. It was a much bigger hospital, in a strange city, and there were changes that needed to be made. I was encouraged to accept by Margaret Fawley and my family, and so I did. I arrived in Leicester on 4 November 1969, my first working day being not only Guy Fawkes Day but also the day of the annual hospital prize-giving. I was just 38. In retrospect, it was not the ideal way of making an appearance – on a platform, with unknown dignitaries, and gawped at by the staff, the prize-winners and their relatives. I felt decidedly foolish. My senior staff made me welcome. Miss Tebbutt, who had been Acting Matron, had deferred her retirement until I arrived and was of the old school – a much-respected disciplinarian with a sense of humour. My "right-hand man" and First Assistant Matron was Maureen Reed, who became a very close friend and was to figure large in our future lives. I also had 2 Assistant Matrons, an Administrative Sister and a Home Sister. I was responsible not only for the satisfactory management of the patients but also for the school of nursing, which was headed by a Nurse Tutor. I was responsible, with Gerald Letts, the Hospital Secretary, to the hospital management committee, but I soon discovered that the committee was a closed shop and instead of taking a full and active part in it, I was only asked to appear for a few items which were thought to be relevant. The same committee also ran the Royal Infirmary in Leicester and it soon became apparent that the RLI was the flagship and the LGH, which had its origins as a workhouse, was very much the poor relation. It also became apparent fairly soon that one or two of the Consultants were "empire building" and trying to use me as a pawn in their power games. All in all, it was not a very happy situation but I tried to make the best of it. Initially, I lived in a house in the grounds, which also housed the 16-year-olds employed on the hospital cadet scheme but I soon realised that I needed more independence. During 1970, I bought a house at the bottom of the hospital drive which had belonged to a retiring Maternity Sister, for less than £2000. It was still difficult at that time for a single woman to get a mortgage but thanks to some securities, I did. Considering that it was 3-bedroomed semi, with a garden, it was a good buy and I was lucky to get on to the housing ladder at that time.

So my first year in Leicester was not too bad. I had excellent secretarial help, good support from the staff, and I particularly enjoyed interviewing staff and recruiting student nurses and following their progress.

Then, following a change of Government, it was decided that, instead of properly evaluating the pilot schemes in place for Salmon, all the recommendations in the report should be implemented nationally, as soon as possible. This decision, in my opinion, was the first great blow to the morale of the NHS and the first of many reorganisations to be inflicted on the staff.

The Sheffield Regional Board became responsible for the major changes in our area and it became apparent that major changes were on their way. A lady was appointed as Chief Nursing Officer to our group, to introduce Salmon, and she was known, and feared, by many. She was a Welsh lady with a sharp tongue, a ruthless streak and friends in high places. During 1971, I was sent a job description for the post of Principal Nursing Officer and invited to apply. There would be several PNOs within the group, all answerable directly to the Welsh dragon. If I applied, the newly-created post would mean that I would lose all control of the school of nursing, and therefore the recruitment of Student Nurses, and instead I would have responsibility for the day-to-day running, not only of Leicester General but also of four small satellite hospitals in the surrounding area. This would mean a great deal of travelling and I would have no extra supporting staff. With misgivings, I applied at the last possible date and after a very long and sticky interview, was offered this new post, and so became a PNO. One of the consequential changes was that the Association of Hospital Matrons could no longer exist, as Hospital Matrons were disappearing fast. This was a shame, as I had enjoyed being a member, meeting colleagues and comparing notes. Instead, up and down the country, bright young men, with little or no relevant experience, were being offered senior posts under the Salmon schemes and the middle-aged spinsters, with years of experience, were being side-lined. It was a time of enormous upheaval and unhappiness and it is not surprising that as morale sank, so levels of stress rose.

I found my new situation extremely difficult, and after several months, it was suggested that I should take sick leave. In fact, that just meant that I had more time to think and brood and worry, and so, in the summer of 1972, I resigned and did what I had always advised others against – I left without a job to go to.

By the time I left Leicester General, I had sold the house for a large profit and moved to Nottingham with Maureen. She had been promoted to a Senior Nursing Officer's post at Nottingham General Hospital and we had decided to pool our resources and buy a house together in a suburb of West Bridgford close to Nottingham. It was a relief to escape from Leicester, which at that time was facing the influx of refugees from Idi Amin's regime.

Nottingham had a good shopping centre and rail bus and road transport was easy. As a matter of urgency, I had to find work. Fortunately, one of my friends was the Matron of a fairly local hospital and while I was considering my future, she offered to employ me as a Midwifery Sister. At least, I was earning, even if my morale was low. How the mighty were fallen! I spent my spare time looking through the local paper for possible employment and was taken by an advertisement from the Nottingham District Land Registry. I did not have a lot to lose, so I applied to be a civil servant. Because of restructuring, there were quite a few vacancies; I was interviewed and offered the post of Clerical Officer. They seemed to be rather amused to be employing a mature person with an unusual background. The pay was very low but the staff were pleasant and helpful and I was trained, with others, to prepare the plans for the conveyancing of property. I was not very artistic and the preparation of drawings, with very precise measurements and colourings, was a great challenge. But I completed the training and was assigned to a team. Despite working with a group of relative youngsters, and being treated rather like a maiden aunt, it was a happy time and a peaceful one after the stormy waters of hospital administration.

However, we had a mortgage to pay and although Maureen was earning good money, and I had reserves, I really needed to increase my income. My first foray into extra money was working as a part-time evening shelf stacker in Sainsbury's. This was undemanding and enjoyable work and the other ladies were easy to work with. During our tea break one evening, one of them asked me what my husband did. When I said I was single, she looked at me and said: "Ee, you jammy bugger!" The blow came when I discovered how much tax I was having to pay on my meagre earnings, so after a few weeks, I gave that up. Next, I acquired a football pool round. The local organiser was very helpful and managed to fiddle the tax so that most of what I earned, I kept. This gave me a fascinating insight in to other people's homes and lives but it was not much fun going out in the evenings when the weather became cold and wet.

Because I was doing quite well in the Land Registry, I was encouraged to apply for promotion, which meant taking Civil Service exams. Again, this involved quite a lot of soul-searching, as I had to decide whether or not I was going to attempt to make a career in the Civil Service at the age of 42. I came to the conclusion that I had little to lose and possibly quite a lot to gain so I gave up the football round and instead embarked on a correspondence course for the Civil Service exams. I had to study primarily English, general knowledge and mathematics. I remembered my dismal School Certificate results but this time I had a purpose. The course took several months to complete and in November 1974, I sat the exams. As ever, it was the maths paper that scared me but I did my best and avoided the questions on algebra!

While waiting for the results, I noticed the post of Assistant Matron being advertised for the Star & Garter Home in Richmond. I saw that a move into the private sector could be a way for me to get back into nursing administration, so I applied and went for an interview. That Christmas was very difficult, as we both had decisions to make. The results of the exams came just before Christmas and I had done much better than I expected. I could be in line for promotion within the Civil Service, with future prospects and a good pension at the end of it. On the other hand, I could return to nursing and make use of the qualifications and experience I had. It was a time of great turmoil, as if I was to go to Richmond, it would mean leaving Nottingham. Which meant that Maureen would either have to stay in Nottingham and keep her job, or move with me and try to find a suitable post in London.

Chapter 10

More Managing and Family

The private sector won, chiefly because the pay was better. But this decision meant leaving the good friends I had made in the Land Registry, it meant returning to greater responsibilities and most of all, it meant leaving Nottingham. I moved down to Richmond in January 1975, living temporarily in staff quarters near the Star & Garter Home, while Maureen continued to work in Nottingham and look after the house and our 3 cats.

The Royal Star & Garter Home, situated at the top of Richmond Hill, was founded after the First World War for the care of returning wounded and disabled servicemen, and had developed over the years into a home for men from all the services, most of whom were suffering from long-term incurable illnesses, like Multiple Sclerosis and Parkinson's Disease. Just a few remained still suffering from the effects of war. Women at that time were not admitted.

It is as well to draw a veil over my relatively short time there as Assistant Matron, as there were major upheavals within the organisation and the politics of management. It was a very difficult time for everyone, staff and residents, and matters were compounded by the increasing power of the trade unions, whose members even went on strike to get their own way, thereby neglecting the essential care of residents. In retrospect, my decision to return to London and my profession was the wrong one. However, we found a terraced house in Kew that we could afford; Maureen, having moved into personnel management, succeeded in obtaining a post at the Royal Free Hospital, Hampstead; and by the end of 1975 we were more or less settled in Kew, one cat having been re-homed in Nottingham, the other 2 having survived the move. Maureen was able to get to work quite easily using the Broad Street Line, which ran from Richmond to the North of London and on round to Liverpool Street station. The house was much smaller that the one we had left in Nottingham and it needed a great deal of basic work doing, but it had a garden and a garage, approached from the rear. We were next to the sewage works, close to the municipal tip and the crematorium, but on the credit side, we were also close to the Thames and London was on our doorstep.

So, as long as I could cope with the stressful problems of very disturbed managers, and one psychotic one, things were not too bad. As a family, we had always had an interest, and faith, in homoeopathy and after a while I consulted a local practitioner in East Sheen. His name was Michael Cox and he had a single-handed NHS Practice as well as a large private practice for homoeopathic patients. I found him approachable, helpful and encouraging, and easy to talk to. But his medicines could not cure the problems at the Star & Garter. I continued to see him every few months but I was quite mystified when one day I received a phone call from him asking me to visit him. When I went, I was very surprised when he asked me if I would consider taking over as his Practice Manager. The prospect was pleasing from many angles – it would get me out of a sticky situation without having to ask for references, stress levels would fall dramatically and I would not have so far to travel. On the debit side were the questions of pay, pension and security, but at the time, these seemed to be relatively minor problems and flattered at being offered a job, I accepted, and for the second time threw up all my training and experience. It was not necessary for a Practice Manager to be a nurse but as it happened, it was very useful.

So, with a certain smug pleasure, I handed in my notice to the Matron at the Star & Garter, leaving shortly after a visit by Her Majesty Queen Elizabeth II, in the autumn of 1976. There followed a peaceful lull in my life, as working for Michael was pleasant and relatively easy, once I had mastered his filing system, conquered the Ansafone and sussed out the few awkward and demanding patients. The practice was busy, open most evenings and every morning except Sundays. One of my first jobs was to elicit the help of one or two likely ladies to provide relief for some evening sessions and occasional Saturdays. I got to know some of the patients very well indeed and looked forward to their visits. The phone certainly presented some problems, as occasionally a disturbed individual would use up all the tape getting profanities and obscenities on the record, leaving no space for genuine callers

HRH The Queen at the Royal Star and Garter Home, Richmond, 1976.

Christmas at Sussindown, 1982, with Mr Espie (Physiotherapist) and Mrs Espie.

or emergencies. Some patients went to extraordinary lengths to try to make an appointment, or bypass me. The surgeries inevitably overran, because above all else, Michael was a good listener, as well as being a supremely good GP. He found it very difficult to keep to schedule and some patients, wanting time themselves, became angry at having to wait, and the atmosphere in the waiting room became more than a little tense at times. The kettle was kept permanently hot. One of my jobs was to keep the waiting room tidy but I put my foot down at having to do the cleaning. I knew how it should be done but I was not prepared to do it myself. There were a few drug addicts on the list, requiring great tolerance and understanding, which fortunately Michael had as I did not. I may still have been addicted to nicotine but I could not empathise with those who took drugs.

All in all, I enjoyed my work, being able, if necessary, to walk to the surgery from our house in Kew. Now that I had a little time on my hands, I started a Foundation Course for the Open University. I had always regretted my lack of a university education and now I welcomed some mental stimulus.

In due course, I managed to submit my essays on time, attend a few tutorials and attend a summer school back in Nottingham. I chose Nottingham so that I could look up old friends but we had very little free time. As it happened, the school coincided with the wedding of Prince Charles and Princess Diana but we learnt, to our horror, that we were expected to work throughout the day. For at least 2 of us, being Royalists, this was too much, so Sue and I devised a wicked plan, whereby Sue was suddenly stricken with headaches and abdominal pain and we felt it was expedient for me, as a trained nurse, to keep an eye on her. This was accepted by the tutors and so I kept one eye on my patient and the other on the television screen which just happened to be in the room. We enjoyed it all very much but we had to keep quiet about the details when in the company of others. Sue made a fairly dramatic recovery as the happy pair went off on their honeymoon.

Despite the wedding, I did not really enjoy the summer school. There was a lot of "role-playing", and re-enacting the problems leading up to the First World War and how it could have turned out differently, but it all gave me a great sense of relief that I was not a full time undergraduate. There was a lot of noise and horseplay, especially in the evenings, and few of the students took it seriously. Nonetheless, I was pleased to hear, later, that I had completed the Foundation Course satisfactorily, and could therefore return to the Open University at some future date for further studies. To date (2004) I don't seem to have had the time!

While my life continued on a fairly even keel, changes had taken place within the family. Patrick and Pauline had divorced, the children never being heard of again. For a while, he continued in Ampleforth but later decided that he wanted to remarry. Although he could remain as a divorced priest, he was unable to continue if he remarried. Consequently, he resigned from Ampleforth, married Valerie and moved to Doncaster where he was able to work as Chaplain to the School for the Deaf. His situation was not a lot easier as, apart from taking on 2 teenage sons, my mother was a frequent visitor. She could not accept Valerie and did her best to disrupt the marriage. Later, Patrick was able to resume parish duties and they moved to Tuxford in Nottinghamshire. This was further for my mother to visit and as my father became more frail, visits became less frequent. I made as many visits to Hull as I could but I kept them short and therefore manageable. My father and I always enjoyed each other's company and shared the same sense of humour, but my mother quickly became jealous if she thought that we were becoming too close. We were all devastated when my father died in March 1985, just a few days before his 83rd birthday. I had seen that he was failing but my mother had been unable to accept that she might lose him. Initially, she was grateful for my help in sorting out her financial affairs. After a year or so of living alone, she sprained her shoulder badly and agreed to going in to a retirement home in Beverley for a couple of weeks' convalescence. She enjoyed the experience so much that she decided to sell up the flat in Hull and become a permanent resident. Patrick, Maureen and I helped her sort out her belongings, sell up and make the move. All was well for 2 or 3 months but then she started to interfere, becoming very involved in other peoples' problems, instructing the staff and demanding her meals at awkward times. I am still horrified to recall that she had been a Samaritan. Eventually, she was asked to leave, in other words, expelled! She had already found an alternative – a nursing home just up the road, where she found the staff pleasant, helpful and accommodating. She moved secretly, one evening, by taxi, without paying her bill. It fell to my lot, on my next visit, to settle up and pour a little oil on the still troubled waters. The Manager of the nursing home bent over backwards to meet her needs, arranging for her, alone,

Father's 80th Birthday, 1982.
Left to right: Patrick, M.E.R., Maureen, E.H.R., R.M.R., Valerie

to have her main meal in the evening. He spoilt her quite a lot, even giving her lifts into Beverley. She was, of course, mentally very alert and intelligent and no doubt she made a bit of a contrast with so many of the residents who were confused. She did not really need a nursing home, as she needed minimal care. However, after a while it became obvious that she was showing psychotic tendencies and she became very argumentative. Whenever I visited, I played countless games of Scrabble with her, as it kept her quiet and took her mind off all the little things which caused her so much irritation. But there came a time when she refused to see me and would not answer letters or take phone calls from me. Patrick, having been out of favour in the past because of his marriage, was now "in", as long as Valerie was not mentioned, and he had to endure increasingly difficult visits. He did not enjoy playing Scrabble and he hated arguments and tensions, but he had to suffer criticisms of me, his wife and the staff of the nursing home who were slowly becoming less accommodating.

Although she had assured me that she would live to at least 100, the end came quite suddenly. It transpired that she had had enough of the nursing home and had moved herself, without telling Patrick or myself, to another nursing home. She had only been there a short while when, at the age of 91, she had collapsed playing Scrabble. She was taken to hospital but died during the night. The hospital phoned me as they could not locate Patrick. I knew that he was on holiday in Derbyshire and at last managed to run him to earth. He was very taken aback, as her demise was so unexpected, but then he told me that he could now go ahead with her obituary notice, which he had been planning for years. It was very short and to the point, and ended with the words: "Peace at last".

After the funeral, Patrick was at last able to enjoy life a little more, particularly gardening, learning Russian and researching the family tree. The four of us used to meet at a halfway point for a pub lunch. We all enjoyed these trips – there was invariably a lot of laughter, especially from the locals when he got his tripod out to record the day. He was always keen on photography. He retired from parish duties, just relieving others during the holidays from time to time. His great sadness was that despite all our efforts, he was never able to make contact with his own children. He had not been particularly fit for some time but it was still an appalling shock when he died, very unexpectedly, while he was on holiday in Llandudno, at the age of 69.

These events were still in the future when I was working for Michael. The only problem I had at that time was raising the embarrassing question of raising my wages. I think he knew just how much it embarrassed me and he used to tease me by prolonging the agony. I had never before been in a situation where I had to negotiate. Nevertheless, I would have stayed working for him if it had not been for a curious co-incidence. One day, Maureen and I drove down to Worthing to meet friends for lunch. They were Olive Kirkham and Iris Keen, both living in Sussex, and both friends from our Air Force days. Having met them, we drove into the country for a pub lunch, passing through Storrington. Olive and Iris pointed out the sign for Sussexdown, a home for disabled men and women of the Air Force. Then I remembered seeing an advertisement for a Matron for Sussexdown and the girls got very excited at the possible prospect of me moving to Sussex and taking the job. As ever, I decided that I had nothing to lose by requesting more information. Having slept on it and discussed it with Maureen and Michael, I applied. I was duly short-listed and interviewed in a London hotel. I did not enjoy the interview at all, being harangued by a senior lady who felt that I was very out of touch with modern nursing practice. I went home with a sense of relief that it was over and was really shocked when the Secretary-General, Frank Neal, rang me the same evening to offer me the post. I then shocked him by saying that I was "gobsmacked", which I was. But I accepted the offer.

Chapter 11
In and Out of Managing

With mixed feelings, I arrived in Storrington in November 1981 but I soon enjoyed being back in a position of responsibility. I was made very welcome by all the staff and worked alongside the retiring Matron for a couple of weeks, before she departed for a life of retirement in Spain. There were 63 residents and people enjoying respite care or a holiday. There were men and women of all sorts and conditions. Some were very severely handicapped and in need of 24-hour care but others were quite independent and just enjoying a break.

I realised very quickly that I was responsible not only for the nursing care but also for the catering, the office girls, the cleaning staff, the gardeners and the maintenance staff. Quite a tall order for one woman of 51 and rather out of touch! But Frank Neal, the Secretary-General of the RAF Association, came down from London quite frequently initially and was extremely helpful, as well as being one of the nicest men I have ever met.

Maureen remained in Kew and continued working at the Royal Free Hospital until we could see the wood for the trees. I was given a flat "over the shop", which was fine in the short term. But there are disadvantages in being always available and one's comings and goings noted by the staff. I tried to get back to Kew at least every 2 weeks because, apart from anything else, Maureen did not drive at that time, which made it difficult for her to get in supplies. We decided that in the Spring, I would start looking for a suitable property, somewhere near a station, so that Maureen could commute to work, staying with friends during the week. As the days lengthened, and when I had a routine well-established, I brought Maureen down to Sussex, so that we could assess the area. We decided, after looking at a number of properties, that we needed to be in Worthing, as the train service to London was good, and at least the places we viewed were on main drainage, which was more than one could say for the rural areas. One Friday in May, after work, I saw a bungalow which seemed to meet our needs. So I dashed up to Kew and we both returned to Worthing in the morning to view it again. But we had lost it overnight. The gentleman from the estate agency, who met us there, was very sympathetic and offered to show us one or two more likely places. We went to one, which I dismissed out of hand because of the very tall Leylandii on one boundary. I thought how dark the garden must be but the long and short of that is that we fell for the bungalow itself and moved in some months later. We eventually had the trees removed and we remained there, very happily, for 15 years.

Meanwhile, at Sussexdown, I settled into a rhythm. My senior staff were pleasant, helpful and supportive but, inevitably, I had problems recruiting staff of the right calibre for the lower grades. It was said that we had exhausted Storrington and yet we were dependent on the local areas. The bus services were far too infrequent to be any use. We did have a staff block, so that ancillary staff could be resident, but eventually we managed to empty it. The fights and affairs all became too much to handle, especially after I interviewed and employed a nubile young Swedish girl. We tried to avoid using agency staff because of the expense but sometimes it was unavoidable.

Sussexdown was maintained mostly by the generosity of people all over the world who belonged to branches of the RAFA. Their efforts at raising money were prodigious. The only disadvantage from my angle was that, understandably, they wanted to visit to see how the funds had been used and they expected me to be present. As sometimes we had branch visits on almost every Saturday and Sunday, it was difficult to have time off. The other disadvantage was that everything donated by a branch ended up with a plaque on it. There were several highlights in the year; one was Swiss Day, when members of the Geneva branch came over round about the New Year with gifts for the residents. Another was Dutch Day, which still continues. Members of the Amsterdam branch fly over, usually in June, and bombard Sussexdown with cheeses, to commemorate the time when the RAF dropped desperately needed supplies to the Dutch at the end of the war. The catering we supplied for these occasions was of the highest quality and always looked very impressive. Dame Vera Lynn usually came to Dutch Day. On one truly memorable occasion, the lads arranged for me to have a trip in a helicopter. It came from Shoreham Airport, landed in the grounds, and whisked me up and over the surrounding countryside.

There were also occasions when we left Sussexdown, sometimes to escort the residents perhaps to a Buckingham Palace garden party or a concert, and sometimes to attend a ball at the Grosvenor Hotel in aid of the RAFA. However, the first time I went to the ball, with my senior staff, I learnt to my horror that we, despite being dressed up to the nines, were expected to deal with any medical emergencies that might arise during the course of the evening. The following year, the St.John's Ambulance Brigade were there at my request and we were able to relax, drink, dance, and enjoy the evening.

I enjoyed my time at Sussexdown, despite the heavy and varied responsibilities thrust upon my shoulders, and I would have remained there until I retired but for an unfortunate incident. I made, to the senior staff at the RAFA Headquarters in Chiswick, what I thought was a cast iron case for an administrative assistant. I thought that if I could have, perhaps, a bright young man to take some of the burden of staff wages, the maintenance of the building, the catering supplies and keeping the grounds looking beautiful for our many visitors off my shoulders, I would be able to concentrate more on the nursing care and the welfare of the residents. By the time I made my case, the staff at Chiswick had changed and Mr Neal, my great help and supporter, had retired. The consequence was that the decision was made, at the highest level, that I had a point and consequently, an *administrator was appointed, over me, to whom I was responsible.* Needless to say, I had no say in the appointment and although I tried to make the new arrangement work, it was very difficult relinquishing authority to someone who did not really have appropriate experience or knowledge. I should have kept my mouth shut, as I brought the change entirely upon myself. It was the worst mistake I made in my life.

After several months of adapting, I started to consider other options to working at Sussexdown. In 1985, I was 54, which is not a good age to make another major change. By this time, Maureen had retired and passed her driving test, so that she was independent. We discussed my dilemma and considered what we might be able to do as a joint exercise. I saw, in the nursing press, an advertisement for something *completely different!* It was to supply clothing to the elderly and disabled, in nursing homes, retirement homes and hospitals, and to individuals in their own homes. We went up to New Malden to discuss the proposition further and learnt that we would buy our stock from the people who ran the business and then have, in effect, a franchise for Sussex. The business was expanding and the 2 brothers who had started it had found that they could no longer cope with the volume of business. But they could give us all manner of help, useful tips and introductions.

So, to the shock of the staff at Sussexdown and HQ, I handed in my notice and left, with some misgivings, in February 1985. My senior staff were aware of the frustrations that I had faced and knew that I had done my best, working ridiculously long hours and never having an opportunity to make up time lost. So the first thing I did was have a 2-week break, doing absolutely nothing. Then we went up to New Malden, bought our stock and started making ourselves known. We supplied a wide range of underwear for men and women, shirts, sweaters, jumpers and cardigans in all sizes, and a good selection of dresses, most of which were easy to put on. We were also able to supply special trousers, made to measure, for severely-disabled men. We were limited in the amount of profit that we could make, as the price list was supplied by the main office in New Malden, and we were not allowed to sell stock obtained from elsewhere. We bought a dress rail, which came apart, and as we became established, we would set off on most days, by appointment, mostly to nursing homes, with the car laden to the roof with black bags containing our stock. We became quite proficient at unloading and setting up in a variety of places, and mostly, we were welcomed and did quite good business. Sometimes, items had to be ordered specially, and on one occasion I was making a return visit to a nursing home in Worthing with some outsize nightdresses when I met the owner. He started chatting, and found out a little about my background and before I realised what was happening, he was offering me the post of Matron, as he was about to sack the present incumbent. That really gave me food for thought. His offer was attractive and there is always something preferable about being employed rather than self-employed. I spent a week or so considering the situation and discussing it but at last gave in and agreed to work for him.

We had only been dealing with clothing for 9 months but we had not made a great deal of money. We were able to find a local couple who were very keen to take it over and in fact they went from strength to strength, later breaking all ties with New Malden and making it a lucrative business.

So on 1 January 1986, I began work as the Matron of St. Michael's Nursing Home and Maureen returned to being a lady of leisure. My boss, who had lured me back, was a charming Iranian and, initially, he gave me a great deal of support and help. At that time, a good nursing home really could not fail and he wanted ours to be the best in Worthing. It certainly had quite a good reputation and we had little difficulty filling beds. I had more difficulty finding enough staff of the right calibre but there was a nucleus of good reliable girls and sometimes they introduced their friends. It was, and is, not much of a job for bright girls and there is not much future in working as a Nursing Auxiliary, but if I could get them as school-leavers, to gain experience before they started their nurse training, it was ideal.

Chapter 12

Into Retirement

I remained at St. Michael's for quite some time but the problems of getting and retaining staff, especially trained staff, remained. Qualified nurses could earn much more with an agency, without having to enter into any long-term commitment to an employer. So who could blame them if they decided to work on their terms. It made things extremely difficult for the Matrons and owners of nursing homes everywhere and it still does. One was dependent on the goodwill of the few members of staff who felt a sense of loyalty to their place of work and their patients.

One day, I heard a rumour of a new nursing home that was being built specifically for the purpose in Walberton, a village between Arundel and Chichester. One evening, I went over to have a look and found a hive of activity as an old house was being completely renovated for nursing home use. This seemed like too good an opportunity to miss – to commission a new business in an area where there were unlimited opportunities for staff. So I applied and went to see Graham and Jean Menzies in their new house in the next village. They had come from Bournemouth, where they had had a rest home, and so they too were venturing into something new. They seemed not to have considered staffing much but were pleased when I offered my services as a Commissioning Matron. Shortly afterwards, this was confirmed and with them, we set about advertising for trained staff, ancillary staff and kitchen, cleaning and gardening staff. I left St. Michaels, my boss being co-operative and understanding, and when we had a nucleus of staff for Walberton, we started looking for potential patients. We had an open day, when the local doctors came to view, as well as possible residents and their relatives. A few weeks later, we officially opened, with one lady. To me, it was an awe-inspiring moment to realise that, from that moment on, there would always be someone to take charge, night and day, for countless years ahead. Other patients followed quite quickly and it was a very exciting time, beginning to operate and realising little things that we had overlooked, like organising a hairdresser for the ladies, finding a chiropodist and realising that the little lift was quite inadequate for the removal of bodies. Inevitably, there were teething troubles, especially in the kitchen when it was discovered that the chef was lazy, often late and unreliable. The Menzies, of course, bore the brunt of the worry of getting ourselves established and they were trying to set up this complicated business at a time when interest rates soared.

They became very depressed and had to rope in various relatives to help with things like laundry and cleaning. They had never appreciated just how many sheets one needs in a nursing home as distinct from a rest home. But gradually things improved, the staff settled down, the number of patients rose and we gathered that we were beginning to get a good name in the area. It was personally a great challenge, that I enjoyed. But it had always been my intention to simply get the new venture well and truly off the ground and after almost 2 years, by which time Walberton Nursing Home was well-established and flourishing, I returned almost inevitably to St. Michaels, once again to try to cope with a staffing crisis. But by 1992, having turned 60, it seemed stupid for me to continue working in a stressful situation when I was in a position to retire.

So, in April of that year, I became a free woman, with all sorts of mad ideas of what I was going to do with the rest of my life. I had a fourfold plan – to do something intellectually stimulating, to undertake some sort of fitness programme, to do something useful for society and to start some activity purely for pleasure.

Things never work out as one plans. Although during the next 10 years or so, we were both confronted with all sorts of totally unexpected and unusual medical problems, Maureen and I also embarked on the fun of travelling. In the past, we had taken coach tours round Italy, Spain and Greece, and package holidays to Cyprus. Now, we were persuaded to join the Friendship Force of Sussex – an international organisation started by Jimmy Carter to break down barriers and create friendships throughout the world. Soon after we joined, we travelled with a group of 23 others to Orange County, in California and spent time in other people's homes. Maureen and I were fortunate enough to stay with a recently-retired teacher who was also new to the organisation and Betty went to great lengths to make it a memorable visit. We met her friends and relatives, visited a shopping mall and spent a whole day at Disneyworld. We had lunch on board the Queen Mary in Long Island and inspected the adjacent Spruce Goose. We met other members of our party from time to time and all in all, had a wonderful week. After the week was up, we changed hosts and we spent another week in San Fernando, north of Los Angeles, where we had an unforgettable week with Jean and Emery Darter and their menagerie of animals. Jean especially was quite eccentric and a shopaholic, but nevertheless, we had an interesting week there and managed to spend a day at Universal Studios.

After this introduction, we became involved not only in hosting ourselves, when groups came over from other countries, but also in day hosting, which meant relieving hosts by taking their guests out for the day and showing them either our beautiful countryside, or castles and churches, or the Lanes in Brighton, according to their interests. After a while, we also undertook the planning of these exchanges, which meant matching visitors to hosts, organising trips out for the day, booking a venue for a farewell meal and generally trying to keep everyone happy. Later in 1991, we went on our second exchange, this time to Tennessee, where we had a week in Memphis followed by a coach trip across the state, via Nashville, to Knoxville for our second week. This was another interesting trip – among other activities, we had a voyage down the Mississippi in a paddle steamer and a snowstorm, and in Knoxville, we were all made Freemen of the City.

As the years passed, we organised several incoming groups, hosted some very interesting and friendly people with whom we still keep in touch, and then in 1994 went off on another trip ourselves. Maureen and I flew from Heathrow to Hong Kong, changing in Bangkok, and after a few days there, we carried on to Auckland in New Zealand. We had time there to look up several contacts and consequently we spent one day being driven around the city and countryside, and on another, we spent the whole day on a ranch south of Auckland. Then, we returned to the airport to meet the rest of our group as they flew in and the New Zealanders who were going to host us for a week. We travelled up to Whangerei by coach and got to know our hosts. We were staying with one of the Merry Widows – 4 ladies who having lost

With the Friendship Forum in Whangerei, New Zealand.
Maureen and I with our N.Z. hostesses Val and Lexie

With Captain Floten on the Black Prince,
cruising to Spitzburgen, June 2000

their husbands had picked up the threads of their lives and carried on. The week we had with them in the North Island was one that we shall never forget. It was a week crammed with good company, wonderful food and some really fantastic experiences, including 8 of us spending 2 nights in a tiny one-bedroom apartment right on the Bay of Islands. We were there for Waitangi Day, Prince Charles being brought ashore by Maori canoe to celebrate the event. We were surrounded by laughter and good humour and we were all very sorry to leave our fantastic hosts in Whangerei.

We all travelled by coach, via Rotorua, where we spent a smelly night, to Wellington, and then took the ferry to Picton on South Island. We journeyed by train to Christchurch, arriving in a thunderstorm. Again, we were met, very warmly, by our hosts and hostesses and taken off to our respective homes. We stayed with Lorna, a stalwart of the organisation, who had been a teacher and was very well travelled. Subsequently, she stayed with us but that is the way things happened with the Friendship Force – one forged links which lasted for years. Our week in and around Christchurch was very enjoyable, though not quite as frenetic as the previous one. We then went our separate ways – some of our group going straight back to Sussex, others seeing more of New Zealand and some going to Bali. We flew to Melbourne to stay with a very old friend who had recently been widowed and after a few days there, flew on to Sydney. We did not expect to like Sydney and consequently we were bowled over by the friendliness, the climate and so many wonderful things to see. Finally, we had a few days in Singapore before returning home after over 6 weeks away.

Before we joined the Friendship Force, I managed to persuade Maureen to try cruising. I had been spoilt by my experiences on ships around the Turkish coast and I was keen to try a British ship. So in 1989 we went to Southampton and boarded Canberra for 2 weeks round the Mediterranean. Unfortunately for our pockets, we caught the cruising bug and proceeded over the next few years to travel 2 or 3 times a year. We experienced all the P&O ships but discovered that we much preferred smaller vessels. All in all, we have enjoyed nearly 20 trips, visiting many ports in the Mediterranean, the Canaries, the Fjords, the Baltic Capitals, the Arctic Circle, the Caribbean and through the Panama Canal to San Francisco via Guatemala and Mexico. In January 2002, we spent over 6 weeks travelling east to Tenerife, the Cape Verde Islands and Walvis Bay in Namibia before going on to Cape

Town, Durban, Mauritius, Singapore, Vietnam, Hong Kong and the Philippines, before calling in to Darwin and travelling down the East Coast of Australia to Sydney.

We have been very lucky to see so much of our world but I feel we can call our travels educational! After the turbulence of my working life, I feel well-compensated by travelling.

In retrospect, I went into the wrong profession. I think I did my best at a very tricky time for the nursing profession and although I have had huge rewards, I have no doubt that I would have been much happier in a different sphere. During the 1970s, I visited a careers consultant and having taken a battery of tests, learnt that I should probably have gone into law. Who knows how my life might have been?

My 70th Birthday lunch. With James.